CAROL CUTLER'S
GREAT FAST BREADS

Books by Carol Cutler

Haute Cuisine for Your Heart's Delight

The Six-Minute Soufflé and Other Culinary Delights

The Woman's Day *Low-Calorie Dessert Cookbook*

Cuisine Rapide

The Woman's Day *Complete Guide to Entertaining*

and *Pâté: The New Main Course for the '80s*
(published by Rawson Associates)

Carol Cutler's
Great Fast Breads

100 CHOICE RECIPES

*Popovers to Panettone
in Two Hours or Less*

RAWSON ASSOCIATES : *New York*

Library of Congress Cataloging in Publication Data

Cutler, Carol.
 Carol Cutler's Great fast breads.

 Includes index.
 1. Title.   II. Title: Great fast breads.
 TX769.C86   1984   641.8'15   84-42538
 ISBN 0-89256-272-2

Published simultaneously in Canada by McClelland and Steward Ltd.
Composition by P&M Typesetting, Inc.
Waterbury, Connecticut
Manufactured by Fairfield Graphics
Fairfield, Pennsylvania
Designed by Jacques Chazaud
Interior artwork by Jackie Aher
First Edition

To Les Dames d'Escoffier

women working in the food and wine industries
who are striving to maintain
the standards of the Master.

Contents

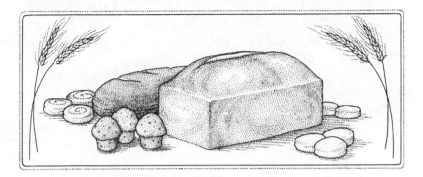

About Fast Breads

America is baking again, and for all the right reasons. We are back to making breads of unsurpassed flavor, nutritious, preservative-free, and costing a mere fraction of those spongy, factory-produced loaves. With the corner bakery almost an extinct species, bread lovers of the nation have no choice but to pull out their baking pans, muffin tins, and dough hooks.

Unfortunately, not everyone who would like to bake has the time or inclination to put in the endless hours usually needed to produce warm, fragrant loaves by the traditional methods. This book is directed to them. Now anyone who has as little as thirty minutes, or two hours at the most, can join in one of the most satisfying of kitchen endeavors. Some of the recipes require *no rising or kneading* and *can be mixed together in as little as ten minutes,* then popped into the oven.

This book is organized by time into four parts: Great Fast Breads in Less Than Thirty Minutes (including time in the oven), Great Fast Breads in Less Than Sixty Minutes, Great Fast Breads in Less Than Ninety Minutes, and Great Fast Breads in Less Than Two Hours. All a reader has to do is decide how much time he or she has and then select a recipe from the appropriate part.

Recipes are included for breads leavened with baking powder, baking soda, beer, egg whites, steam, and yeast. Some are not leavened at all. The most exciting recipes use the new fast yeasts, which cut rising time in half. They made many good breads eligible for this book that otherwise would have failed to meet the two-hour deadline. Even with fast-rising yeasts, new preparation methods had to be developed for some recipes to save even more time without sacrificing taste. These new methods are clearly spelled out in the text and will allow readers to develop their own shortcut recipes.

One brand-new yeast bread—No-Knead, No-Rise Buttermilk Bread—was born of a serendipitous mistake. It is rare in that, as the title states, it requires no kneading and no rising. From the instant the package of yeast is opened, you spend *a scant ten minutes* before popping the bread pan into the oven, which may be a record for this type of bread. This bread is so successful that I developed three other versions of it.

The opening part is, of necessity, limited to what are known as quick breads, but they do not have to be banal. In addition to classics such as Baking Powder Biscuits, you will find such unexpected treats as Pumpkin Muffins, Jelly Buns, Jiffy Fruit Muffins, and onion-laden Oatmeal Panbread. More recipes are given in the part on sixty-minute breads than any other. You will be pleasantly surprised to see what spectacular breads can be made in a total of less than one hour. Although yeast is occasionally used in the first two parts, it is a major ingredient in breads taking approximately ninety minutes. Here you will also find the new no-knead, no-rise breads, as well as several types of sandwich loaves, plain and flavored popovers, and French loaves. Among the last recipes in the book are those for delightful swirled breads, puffy *Panettone,* an innovative quick German *Stollen* in both sweet and savory versions, and still others that encase chili peppers, sausage, cottage cheese, and jam.

These pages contain recipes for many kinds of breads—rolls, muffins, flatbreads, fried breads, and steamed breads, as well as a wide choice of regular and sweetened yeast breads. Sweet breads are placed at the end of each part because they play a different role, generally being enjoyed by themselves with a hot drink, rather than as part of a meal. I also deliberately have included a variety of preparation methods in each part to meet the baking preferences of different readers. For example, there are yeast breads that take no kneading; some are whirled in the food processor; still others call for kneading, a therapeutic procedure that many people find calms their frazzled nerves. Anytime a food processor is called for in the recipe, that fact is indicated in the title to allow those without the machine to move on to another recipe. All food-processor breads are paired with another version for which the device is not needed. Although I have not specified a dough hook, anyone who has one certainly could use it instead of kneading by hand.

The flavors of these 100 recipes come from around the world, providing a cornucopia of taste sensations that no grocery shelf can match. Now brought together for the baker in a hurry are specialties like Scandinavian Whole Wheat Flatbread, Irish Soda Bread, Armenian Seed Crackers, Italian Bread Sticks and *Panettone, Lefse* (Norwegian Potato Flatbread), English Scones and Muffins, *Chappati* (Indian Whole Wheat Flatbread), German Pumpernickel, and *Stollen.* Other quick recipes have no further history than my kitchen. Now, let's make bread and break bread!

Fast-Rising Yeasts

For anyone who wants to make bread in a hurry, the new fast-rising yeasts are a boon. They reduce rising time by half and have made it possible to include a number of breads that otherwise would have had to be left out of this book. The two major manufacturers of fast-rising dry yeast are Red Star and Fleischmann's. Each brand of yeast is excellent, but each has different properties that prevent their use interchangeably. The major difference is in proofing—mixing the dry yeast with liquid to rehydrate it and start yeast cell growth. This can be done with Red Star but is not recommended by Fleischmann's.

Fleischmann's fast-rising yeast has a thinner cellular structure that necessitates its being mixed with dry ingredients, principally flour, and adding water heated to 125 to 130 degrees Fahrenheit. In most homes in which energy conservation and cost are a concern, hot water heaters are set between 115 and 120 degrees, the ideal temperature for proofing yeast. Heating water in a pot to a higher temperature is simple enough, but once heated to 130 degrees, liquids will skyrocket to 140 to 150 degrees in a flash. This excessive heat kills yeast. I pondered whether readers who decide to bake bread on the spur of the moment would bother to check the temperature of the water with a thermometer, or be patient enough to wait for the overheated liquid to cool. I decided some might not.

Therefore, the majority of yeast recipes in this book have been developed with Red Star fast-rising yeast, which can be proofed with ordinary hot tap water. For other recipes, in which the dry yeast is mixed with the flour, either brand can be used. Any reader can elect to use the nonproofing method and simply add the yeast to the flour, following with the liquid heated to 125 to 130 degrees. The choice is personal.

Note: When a recipe calls for *proofable fast-rising yeast,* use Red Star; when a recipe says *fast-rising yeast,* either Fleischmann's or Red Star can be used.

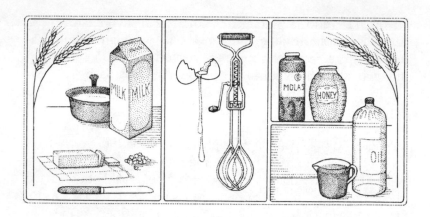

Bread-Baking Tips

Yeast Breads

Yeast terms:

Proof—Mixing crumbled fresh yeast or dry yeast granules with warm water (115 degrees Fahrenheit) and other ingredients, usually sugar and a spice, to allow the yeast to begin reactivating and growing. When put aside in a warm spot for as little as five minutes, the yeast will grow in volume and become foamy. When adding the proofed yeast to a batter always scrape in every bit of it with a rubber spatula.

Sponge—A thick batter that is a combination of the proofed yeast and flour. Sometimes the flour is added at the beginning, at other times after the yeast has become foamy.

Rise—The increase in volume of the dough as the yeast cells increase their production of carbon dioxide gas, which stretches the gluten mesh. Rising is always done in a warm atmosphere, 80 to 85 degrees Fahrenheit for these breads. Some recipes in this book are given one rise, others two, and still others none.

Where to Rise—A gas oven with a pilot light works perfectly. To use an electric oven, turn it on to 110 degrees for one minute, place the dough in the oven and after ten seconds turn off the heat. One can also use the top of the stove with one or two burners turned on to low. If the stove surface feels too hot, slip a wooden board under the bowl. Radiators are fine in the wintertime, but put a board under the bowl. Even hot water can be used—put the bowl with dough in a larger bowl partially filled with hot water and stretch plastic wrap over the two bowls.

Fast-Rising Yeasts—Both Red Star and Fleischmann's produce fast-rising yeasts, which are used exclusively in this book. The yeasts come in one-quarter-ounce packages that measure out to two teaspoons. The teaspoon quality is always listed for precision. The differing qualities of the two yeasts are discussed on page 5.

Salt and Sugar and Fats and Yeast—Salt and fats retard the growth of yeast cells. A little bit of sugar encourages growth, but too much retards cell development. For these reasons, follow the directions carefully. Don't think that if a little bit of sugar will give a boost, a whole lot will be like jet propulsion; it doesn't work that way. To encourage yeast growth and gluten development, many of these recipes add the salt, additional sugar, and fat at different stages of the preparation.

Spices with Yeast—Don't ignore the inclusion of a pinch of spice (ginger, mace, nutmeg, cinnamon, or others) when proofing the yeast. The spice provides extra food to get the yeast growing quickly.

Yeast Clumps—Don't worry if some of the yeast granules clump together after the water has been added. They are pasty and moist, which means they are already rehydrated and working.

Yeast Storage—Packets of unopened yeast should remain fresh for at least twelve months if stored in a cool, dry place. I keep mine in the refrigerator, removing enough for one baking spree in time for it to reach room temperature. Always use the yeast before the expiration date printed on the package.

Protecting the Dough—To prevent the rising dough from drying and forming a crust, cover the bowl. Plastic wrap works very well. I also like a heavy dish towel soaked in hot water and wrung out, then draped over the bowl. Aluminum foil is not as good because it easily absorbs any itinerant cool breeze. A small glass of water placed in the oven while the dough is rising also helps prevent any drying of the dough's surface.

Temperature—All ingredients should be brought to room temperature.

Cold Eggs—For yeast breads cold eggs can be warmed under the hot water tap for ten seconds or so; or immerse them in a bowl of lukewarm water for a few moments.

Warm Water—Most yeast recipes specify warm water. This means between 115 and 120 degrees Fahrenheit. Water from the hot water tap in most kitchens is in this temperature range. Check your hot water with a thermometer, and feel the water to become familiar with it. Water at these temperatures feels hot to the hand but not uncomfortably so.

Temperature Testing—When taking a thermometer reading of a heating liquid, make certain the thermometer is not resting on the hot bottom of the pot but is suspended *in the center of the liquid.*

Cooling Hot Liquids—To cool overheated liquids, pour them back and forth between two pans or bowls or suspend the pot in a large bowl filled with cold water.

Bread Flour—With the current baking revival in the United States, bread flour is no longer an exotic product. It is on most supermarket shelves right beside regular flours. If you can't find it, use all-purpose flour in the recipe but allow a little extra rising time.

Baking Powder Breads

Overbeating—Baking powder batter should be beaten only long enough to blend all the ingredients. Overbeating will produce smaller, heavier loaves.

Cracks—Cracks belong there, right on top, and are characteristic of baking powder breads. You did not make any mistakes.

Cooling Baked Loaves—Baking powder breads are more delicate than yeast breads. They must cool in the pan for about ten minutes before unmolding to allow the steam to subside and the interior of the loaf to firm a little.

Slicing—These breads slice best when completely cooled; a serrated bread knife works best.

General Tips

Measuring Flour—To measure flour, first spoon the flour into a measuring cup until overflowing, then level off with a knife. When a recipe specifies "sifted flour" it means the flour should be sifted first, then measured as described above.

Greasing Pans—I usually just use the word "grease" in instructions to coat the mold with a fat. The reason is that fats are interchangeable. I almost always use vegetable oil because it coats the pan most thoroughly. It is 100 percent fat and when smeared over the interior leaves no half-greased spots. Butter or margarine can also be used, but I do not recommend lard because its flavor might not be compatible with the bread. Following usual recipe practice, quantities needed for greasing pans usually are not specified in the list of ingredients.

Rye and Whole Wheat Flours—If these flours are not used often, keep them in the refrigerator or freezer. They still contain the wheat germ, which has fat that can become rancid. For yeast breads allow the flour to come to room temperature before using. Both flours can be found on supermarket shelves or in health food stores.

Diced Butter—Many recipes specify that butter be cut into pieces even when it will be melted in a hot liquid. The reason is to minimize liquid evaporation. A solid chunk of cold butter will take much longer to melt than small pieces; in the meantime the level of liquid is reduced and recipe proportions can be thrown off.

Cold Milks—If the milk or buttermilk used in the recipe should be room temperature, it can be warmed quickly by pouring the amount needed into a bowl or pot and placing it over a pot filled with hot water.

Honey and Molasses—When measuring these viscous ingredients, oil the measuring cup or spoon first to help the sugary syrup slide off, leaving no residue and ensuring an accurate measure.

Grated Lemon and Orange Rinds—Reserve a stiff-bristled kitchen brush for brushing the grated rind from between the teeth of small graters.

Food Processor—Always use the steel blade.

Muffin Tins—If all the muffin cups in a muffin tin are not filled, pour water into the empty ones to protect the metal.

Loaf Pans—Black metal loaf pans which absorb heat and produce a crisper crust are the best vehicle for baking yeast breads. Generally they measure 11 × 5 × 3½ inches and taper a little toward the bottom. Ovenproof glass loaf pans are usually straight-sided and measure a little smaller than metal ones. I prefer glass dishes for baking powder breads.

Egg Whites—Egg whites that are to be beaten should always be at room temperature. When beating a small quantity of whites a good rotary hand beater is the best instrument; an electric beater is too fast.

Dried Fruits and Nuts—Unless used fairly quickly, they are best kept in the freezer. Nuts, especially, can become rancid because of their high fat content.

Testing for Doneness—The most common method for testing yeast breads is to turn the loaf out of the pan, rap it on the bottom, and listen for a hollow sound. For nonyeast breads, the testing is usually done by plunging a toothpick, skewer, or thin knife into the center; it should emerge dry unless the recipe specifies otherwise.

Storing Breads—Once cooled, breads should be wrapped in plastic wrap and kept at room temperature; the refrigerator tends to dry them out. Any breads containing meat or fresh cheeses, such as cottage cheese or ricotta, should be refrigerated. I have found that most breads freeze well if carefully wrapped to be airtight. Preslicing allows you to remove several slices of bread while the remainder stays frozen.

PART ONE

Great Fast Breads
in Less Than Thirty Minutes

Great Fast Breads
in Less Than Thirty Minutes

Scones

English scones are kissing cousins to American baking powder biscuits. On each side of the Atlantic there are differing
ideas about whether to hand shape or roll the dough. To my
mind, hand shaping results in a lighter product. Always handle the dough delicately and as little as possible.

Makes about eighteen 2-inch scones

> 4 cups all-purpose flour
> 1 teaspoon baking soda
> 2 teaspoons cream of tartar
> 1 teaspoon salt
> 4 tablespoons butter, room temperature, cut into pieces
> 2 eggs
> 1¼ cups buttermilk

Preheat oven to 400 degrees.

1. Stir all dry ingredients—flour, baking soda, cream of tartar, and salt—together in a large mixing bowl. Add the butter
pieces and rub in with the back of a fork. Beat the eggs in a
small bowl, add the buttermilk, and pour this liquid over the
flour mixture. Stir briefly with a fork, then knead for a few
seconds in the bowl. The dough will be soft; let it rest for 5
minutes.

2. Lightly flour your hands. Break off pieces of dough
about the size of a large egg, roll into a ball between your
palms, put down on a greased baking sheet, and flatten the
top a little. If the dough is sticky, pat it with a wad of plastic
wrap. Leave at least 1 inch of space between the scones.

3. Bake for 10 to 15 minutes or until the scones have
puffed and turned a light golden color. Serve hot.

Baking Powder Biscuits

High school cooking classes usually include biscuits in one of the very early lessons. The logic behind that choice is simple—biscuits are just about the easiest and quickest rolls in the world to prepare because the less you do to them, the better. Variations on the standard biscuit go on and on. A wetter batter is dropped onto a baking sheet by spoonfuls, richer batters replace some of the milk with egg, and still others eschew butter and milk completely and use rich whipping cream. The inclusion of cheese, onions, herbs, or poppy seeds can completely change the character of the biscuit. No matter what you want to do with these hot rolls, they start here.

Makes ten to twelve 2½-inch biscuits

    2 cups all-purpose flour
    1 tablespoon baking powder
    ½ teaspoon salt
    ¼ cup cold butter, cut into pieces
    about ¾ cup milk

Preheat oven to 450 degrees.

1. In a mixing bowl combine the flour, baking powder, and salt. Add the butter and cut it into the flour with a pastry blender or two knives. Work the butter until it is reduced to tiny bits and the mixture has a granular look. Slowly pour in the milk while stirring with a fork; do not pour all the milk

at once. The amount needed will depend on the protein quality of the flour, which means some flours absorb more liquid than others. Gather the dough in the bowl and gently knead it for a few seconds, only long enough to produce a cohesive ball.

2. On a lightly floured board either pat or gently roll the dough until it is about ½-inch thick. Cut into 2-inch rounds with a cookie cutter or glass tumbler and place on an ungreased baking sheet. Reassemble the extra dough, lightly knead together, and proceed as above until all the dough has been used.

3. Bake for about 12 minutes or until the biscuits are a very pale gold. Place in a napkin-lined basket and serve at once.

Buttery Biscuits

The combination of two leavenings—baking powder and yeast—produces an especially tasty and airy biscuit. A golden, buttery crust is achieved by dipping the cut biscuits in melted butter. If you prefer, the butter bath can be eliminated; the biscuit will be equally good but the crust will be drier. Do not attempt to prepare these biscuits in the food processor unless you like heavy rolls.

Makes about sixteen 2-inch biscuits

> 1 teaspoon proofable fast-rising yeast
>   *(see yeast note, page 5)*
> 1 tablespoon sugar, plus ¼ teaspoon
> 2 tablespoons warm water
> about 3 cups all-purpose flour
> 2 teaspoons baking powder
> ½ teaspoon salt
> 8 tablespoons (1 stick) butter, diced
> 1 cup buttermilk, room temperature
> 8 tablespoons (1 stick) butter, melted

Preheat oven to 400 degrees.

1. In a small cup mix the yeast, ¼ teaspoon sugar, and the warm water and put aside in a warm spot. Sift together into a mixing bowl 3 cups flour, 1 tablespoon sugar, baking powder, and salt. Cut the diced butter into the flour with a pastry blender or two knives until the mixture looks mealy.

2. Scrape the yeast into the buttermilk and stir. Pour the liquid over the dry ingredients and stir with a fork just until the mixture is well blended. Gather the dough into a ball and place on a floured board. Pat the dough with the palms of your hands until about ½-inch thick. Flour your hands if necessary.

3. Pour the melted butter into a wide saucer. Cut out 2-inch round biscuits, as directed in the previous recipe. Place each biscuit on a fork, quickly dip into the melted butter, and hold the biscuit above the saucer for a few seconds to allow excess butter to drip off. Place the buttered biscuit on a very lightly oiled baking sheet. (There will be a good deal of melted butter left over, but this quantity is necessary for the butter bath. Refrigerate what remains and use it for sautéing.) Alternatively, dip only the bottom of the biscuit in the butter and, after all the biscuits are on the baking sheet, paint the tops with the melted butter.

4. Gather scraps of dough together, pat out again, and continue to cut and dip. Bake for about 15 minutes or until the biscuits are dry to the touch and lightly golden in color.

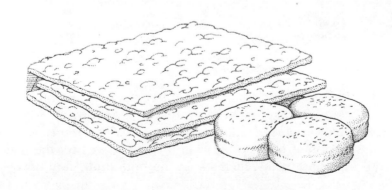

Three-Flour Muffins

Actually, cornmeal doesn't qualify as a flour, but literary license was taken to simplify the title. I wanted all three of these grains for a like number of reasons. Cornmeal contributes a little crunch, whole wheat imparts its slightly nutty flavor, and good old dependable all-purpose flour is there for its rising properties. Add a little molasses and you have a very interesting muffin.

Makes twelve 2½-inch muffins

> ½ cup whole wheat flour
> ½ cup all-purpose flour
> 1 teaspoon baking powder
> 1 teaspoon baking soda
> ¼ teaspoon salt
> 1 cup yellow cornmeal
> 1 egg
> 1 cup buttermilk
> ¼ cup molasses

Preheat oven to 425 degrees.

1. Either grease a muffin tin or place paper-lined foil cups on a baking sheet. Sift together into a mixing bowl the whole wheat and all-purpose flours, baking powder, baking soda, and salt. Stir in the cornmeal. In a small bowl beat the egg until light and frothy, then stir in the buttermilk, and finally the molasses.

2. Pour the liquid ingredients into the mixing bowl and stir gently with a wooden spoon just until all the ingredients are thoroughly blended. Do not overmix or the muffins will be tough. Spoon the batter into the muffin cups just to the two-thirds level. Place in the oven at once and bake for about 15 minutes or until a toothpick plunged into the center comes out clean. Cool the muffins in the cups for 5 minutes, then gently ease them out. A grapefruit knife works beautifully. Serve hot.

Pumpkin Muffins

These muffins can easily be adapted to make a more dessert-like roll by doubling the sugar and adding raisins, nuts, and vanilla. For a bread roll, though, I prefer these proportions.

Makes about sixteen 2½-inch muffins

> 2 cups all-purpose flour
> ½ cup dark brown sugar, well packed
> 2 teaspoons baking soda
> ½ teaspoon salt
> ¼ teaspoon cinnamon
> ¼ teaspoon nutmeg
> ¼ teaspoon ginger
> 1 cup puréed pumpkin
> 2 tablespoons honey
> ½ cup oil
> ½ cup water
> 1 tablespoon rum

Preheat oven to 350 degrees.

1. Oil muffin tins or arrange paper-lined foil cups on a baking sheet. In a mixing bowl stir together all the dry ingredients: flour, brown sugar, baking soda, salt, cinnamon, nutmeg, and ginger. In a separate bowl beat together the pumpkin, honey, oil, water, and rum. Pour the pumpkin mixture over the flour and seasonings and mix with a wooden spoon to combine all the ingredients.

2. Spoon the batter into the muffin cups to the two-thirds level and bake for about 15 to 20 minutes or until they feel firm and a toothpick plunged into the center comes out clean.

Ice-Cream Muffins

That's right, these muffins are made with ice cream as the base. The only hint of their unusual beginning is the faint taste of vanilla. The ice cream also brings other attributes—a very fluffy texture and a shiny, golden surface that is self-made.

Makes twelve 2½-inch muffins

> 1 pint vanilla ice cream
> 1 egg
> 2 tablespoons oil
> 1½ cups all-purpose flour
> 1 tablespoon baking powder
> 1 teaspoon salt

Preheat oven to 425 degrees.

1. Oil a muffin tin or arrange paper-lined foil cups on a baking sheet. Put the ice cream in a mixing bowl and let it soften a little. Beat the egg and oil together in a small bowl and stir into the ice cream. Sift the flour, baking powder, and salt over the ice-cream base and stir with a wooden spoon until all the ingredients are well blended.

2. Fill the cups to the three-quarter level and bake for about 20 minutes or until golden brown on top and a toothpick plunged into the center comes out clean.

Skillet Corn Bread

By preheating the heavy cast-iron skillet the cook guarantees a very crisp and brown crust. Any heavy skillet can be used, but its handle must be able to withstand the high oven temperature.

Makes one 10-inch round bread

> 1½ cups yellow or white cornmeal
> ½ cup all-purpose flour
> 1 tablespoon baking powder
> 1 tablespoon sugar
> 1 teaspoon salt
> 2 eggs
> 2 tablespoons melted butter or bacon drippings
> 1½ cups buttermilk

Preheat oven to 400 degrees.

1. In a bowl stir all the dry ingredients together until thoroughly blended. In another bowl beat together the eggs, butter, and buttermilk and pour over the cornmeal mixture. Stir the batter with a fork until all the ingredients are thoroughly blended, but do not overmix.

2. Thoroughly coat a 10-inch cast-iron skillet with oil and place in the preheated oven for several minutes or until smoking hot. Carefully remove the skillet from the oven, pour in the batter, and smooth the surface. Bake for 20 to 25 minutes or until the top is lightly browned and the bread begins to pull away from the sides of the skillet. Cut into wedges and serve at once.

Corn Dodgers

Various corn breads and their unusual names are discussed on page 27. Corn Dodgers clearly belong among the oddly named breads, but they appear here because they are prepared and baked in less than thirty minutes. Besides, as much as I searched, I could not find a plausible explanation for the name. Any suggestions?

White cornmeal is traditional, but yellow can also be used.

Makes about twenty small cakes

> ½ cup butter, diced
> 1¼ cups water
> 1¾ cups white cornmeal
> 1 teaspoon salt

Preheat oven to 450 degrees.

1. Combine the butter and water in a small pot, put on medium heat, and bring to a boil, stirring occasionally. Meanwhile, measure the cornmeal and salt into a mixing bowl and grease a baking sheet with oil. As soon as the butter is melted, pour the hot liquid over the cornmeal and stir with a wooden spoon until the mixture turns into a thick mush. Stir for a few minutes to cool the batter so as to allow it to firm a little and maintain its shape.

2. Drop the batter by spoonfuls onto the baking sheet and place in the oven for about 20 minutes or until the mounds have taken on a very pale gold color and are crisp on the outside. Serve hot, but remember, the sizzle you heard when the oven door was opened is still inside the little cakes; when fresh from the oven, eat with care.

Oatmeal Panbread

The original version of this homespun bread can be found in that treasure of a book, *Everyday Cooking with Jacques Pepin.* In good country-style cooking, the recipe calls for one cup of *grated* onions. For me that means a lot of crying, so I reworked Jacques's instructions and put all the ingredients through a food processor. His list of ingredients specified quick oatmeal. I tried it with both quick and regular. He's right; the texture is smoother with the faster oatmeal, but many people might prefer the slight crunchiness produced with the regular variety. This emphatically flavored bread is baked in a skillet and is a hearty accompaniment with light meals.

Makes one 8-inch flatbread (1¼ pounds)

> ½ cup milk
> 1 medum onion, cut into chunks
> 1 egg
> ½ teaspoon salt
> ¼ teaspoon freshly ground black pepper
> 1 cup quick oatmeal
> 2 teaspoons double-acting baking powder
> ½ cup parsley
> 3 tablespoons oil

Preheat oven to 400 degrees.

1. Into the bowl of a food processor put the milk, onion, egg, salt, and pepper. Process until the onion is completely

puréed. Add the oatmeal and the baking powder and process until they are incorporated into the purée. Finally, add the parsley and process briefly, just enough to chop it a little.

2. Heat 2 tablespoons of the oil in a 7- or 8-inch heavy iron skillet. When the oil is hot, pour in the batter and spread the last tablespoon of oil on top. Bake for 15 or 20 minutes or until you can see the edges turn brown.

3. Flip the bread over to brown the other side. This is most easily done by inverting a plate or flat lid over the skillet, turning them over together, and sliding the bread back into the skillet. Handle the hot skillet with great care and plenty of pot holders. Bake for another 5 minutes and slide onto a plate. Cool for 2 or 3 minutes and slice into wedges.

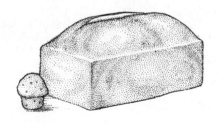

Pumpkin Harvest Loaf

Pumpkin, cornmeal, and molasses are all associated with the cooler months of the year, hence the name, but this bread can be enjoyed anytime. It has an emphatic flavor, so slice it thin.

Makes one 8 × 4 × 2½-inch loaf (1½ pounds)

5 tablespoons butter
1 cup flour
1 cup yellow cornmeal
1 tablespoon baking powder
½ teaspoon baking soda
1 teaspoon salt
½ cup pumpkin purée
1 egg
1 cup milk
¼ cup molasses
1 tablespoon rum

Preheat oven to 400 degrees.

1. Melt the butter and put aside. Cut a piece of parchment or wax paper to fit the bottom of a loaf pan, preferably one of ovenproof glass. Oil the pan, place the paper on the bottom, flip it over, and push down flat. Sift together directly into a mixing bowl the flour, cornmeal, baking powder, baking soda, and salt.

2. Put the pumpkin purée into another bowl, add the melted butter, and combine with a whisk. Add the egg and

beat well. Finally, add the remaining ingredients—milk, molasses, and rum—and blend well.

3. Pour the pumpkin mixture over the dry ingredients and stir just until all the ingredients are well mixed; this should not take more than a minute.

4. Pour the batter into the prepared loaf pan and bake for 15 to 20 minutes or until a toothpick plunged into the center comes out clean and the top has cracked a little. Cool for 10 minutes in the pan, turn out, pull off the paper, and cool on a rack.

Scandinavian Flatbread

This extremely thin flatbread is an example of the good breads the Scandinavians have been enjoying for so long. It is best when served warm, right out of the oven, but can also be cut into wedges and reheated in a toaster oven.

Makes one thin 10-inch round

> 2 teaspoons oil
> ⅓ cup buttermilk
> ⅓ cup heavy cream
> 1 tablespoon butter, melted
> ½ teaspoon salt
> ½ teaspoon sugar
> ⅓ cup rye flour
> ⅓ cup whole wheat flour

Preheat oven to 450 degrees.

1. Grease a cast-iron skillet with the oil. In a mixing bowl stir together all the ingredients in the order listed. Scrape the batter into the skillet and spread into a thin, even layer with a spatula.

2. Bake the flatbread for about 10 minutes or until the edges turn brown and begin pulling away from the skillet. The flatbread can be slipped out of the skillet onto a round serving dish or turned upside down onto a dish to present a darker crust. I prefer the duskier presentation. Cut into wedges.

Whole Wheat Flatbread

This disk of flatbread has much in common with many Scandinavian breads, though rye flour is usually incorporated into the Nordic versions. Despite its speed of preparation, Whole Wheat Flatbread makes no compromises in flavor.

Makes one 12-inch flatbread

>   1½ cups whole wheat flour
>   1 teaspoon baking powder
>   ½ teaspoon salt
>   ¾ cup water
>   2 tablespoons butter, melted
>   2 tablespoons wheat germ
>   2 tablespoons sesame seeds

Preheat oven to 400 degrees.

1. Select a 12-inch pizza pan, heavy round griddle, or skillet and lightly oil it. In a mixing bowl stir together the flour, baking powder, and salt. Add the water and stir with a wooden spoon to make a soft dough.

2. Scoop the dough onto the prepared pan and with your hands press it into a large, flat round. You may find it necessary to moisten your hands with cold water to prevent the dough from sticking to them. Sprinkle the melted butter over the top with a tablespoon and use the back of the spoon to spread the butter all over the surface.

3. In a cup combine the wheat germ and sesame seeds, then sprinkle this mixture over the top of the bread. Bake until the bread is brown, firm, and begins to pull away from the edges of the pan. Serve warm or remove to a rack to cool. This flatbread freezes perfectly.

Blueberry Muffins

Muffins are perhaps the easiest quick breads to make. The less you do to the batter, the better. Use just a few swift strokes to incorporate dry and liquid ingredients—and stop. Overbeating will develop the gluten in the flour and produce tough muffins. Fresh blueberries are incomparably superior to frozen, but since we can't have them all year around, use the frozen rather than foregoing this delightful addition to the bread basket. Do not use canned berries.

Makes sixteen 2½-inch muffins

> 2 cups all-purpose flour
> ⅔ cup sugar
> 1 tablespoon baking powder
> ¼ teaspoon nutmeg
> ½ teaspoon salt
> 1 cup blueberries
> 2 eggs
> ½ cup milk
> ½ cup butter, melted

Preheat oven to 400 degrees.

1. Grease muffin tins or arrange paper-lined foil cups on a baking sheet. Sift the flour, sugar, baking powder, nutmeg, and salt into a mixing bowl. Add the blueberries and stir lightly to coat them with flour. If using frozen berries, partially defrost them.

2. In a small bowl beat together the eggs, milk, and butter; pour over the contents in the bowl and stir briefly with a fork, just until the liquid and dry ingredients are blended. Fill the muffin cups to the two-thirds level and tap the tin on the counter once or twice to settle the batter into the bottom of each cup. Bake at once. When the muffins are puffed and golden brown they are baked, about 15 minutes. Allow the muffins to cool in the tins for 5 minutes before removing. Serve hot.

Orange-Raisin Muffins

Though these muffins have a sunny color, sparkling fra-
grance, and delicious flavor, they are still child's play to
make. There is one great plus to preparing them for breakfast—the aroma from the oven will get everyone to the table
in a hurry. Although white or dark raisins can be used, for
color harmony, I favor the lighter.

Makes about sixteen 2½-inch muffins

> 2 cups all-purpose flour
> ½ cup sugar
> ½ teaspoon salt
> 1¼ teaspoons baking soda
> 1 teaspoon grated orange rind
> 1 cup orange juice
> ½ cup oil
> 1 teaspoon vanilla
> ½ cup raisins tossed with 1 tablespoon flour

Preheat oven to 375 degrees.

1. Grease muffin tins or arrange paper-lined foil cups on
a baking sheet. Measure into a mixing bowl the flour, sugar,
salt, and baking soda. Add the grated orange rind and stir
with a whisk to mix all the dry ingredients.

2. In a small bowl stir together the orange juice, oil, and
vanilla and pour over the dry ingredients. Whisk thoroughly
to blend all the ingredients. Add the raisins and spoon the
batter into the muffin cups just to the two-thirds level and
bake for about 20 minutes or until the tops are puffed and
golden brown and a toothpick plunged into the center
comes out clean. Cool on a rack for a few minutes and serve
warm.

Jiffy Fruit Muffins

These muffins carry no particular fruit title because that depends on what you have in the refrigerator or on the pantry shelf. The moist muffins can be made with nuggets of fresh fruit such as apricots, peaches, cherries, or bananas. Frozen or canned pineapple, peaches, apricots, or even fruit cocktail can be pressed into service when you feel a sudden urge for a different kind of roll.

Makes twelve 2-inch muffins

> ¾ cup fruit pieces
> ¼ cup vegetable shortening or softened butter
> ⅓ cup sugar
> 2 tablespoons honey
> 1 cup all-purpose flour
> 1 teaspoon baking soda
> ¼ teaspoon salt
> ½ cup wheat germ
> 1 egg
> ⅔ cup light cream
> ½ teaspoon vanilla

Preheat oven to 375 degrees.

1. If using canned fruit, drain it very well. Frozen fruit should be partially defrosted. Grease a muffin tin or place paper-lined foil cups on a baking sheet. Cream the shortening or butter with the sugar and honey. Sift the flour, baking soda, and salt into the bowl. Add the wheat germ and stir.

2. Beat together in a small bowl the egg, cream, and vanilla and pour over the creamed ingredients. Mix to blend all ingredients, then carefully fold in the fruit.

3. Fill the muffin cups two-thirds full and bake for about 15 minutes or until they are puffed and golden brown.

Jelly Buns

Odds and ends of jams and jellies can be put to admirable use in these crisp little rolls.

Makes about sixteen 3-inch buns

½ cup milk
3 cups all-purpose flour
1 teaspoon baking powder
1 teaspoon salt
½ cup wheat germ
8 tablespoons butter, cut into pieces
2 eggs
about ⅓ cup jam or jelly

Preheat oven to 400 degrees.

1. Warm the milk to lukewarm and pour into a small bowl. Grease a baking sheet. Sift the flour, baking powder, and salt into a mixing bowl. Stir in the wheat germ, then cut the butter into the flour with a pastry blender or two knives. Work the mixture until it is mealy. Add the eggs to the milk and beat together, then pour over the dry ingredients and stir with a fork until the batter holds together.

2. Pull off pieces of dough about the size of a golf ball and roll between your palms into a ball. Place the balls on a baking sheet about 1½ inches apart. With the back of a teaspoon or a large thimble, make a depression in the center of each dough roll. Slip a scant teaspoon of jelly into each well, pull the dough up over the filling, and pinch together to encase it. While covering the jelly, work the dough into an oval shape; the rolls will resemble a miniature football. Bake for 10 to 12 minutes or until the buns are brown and crisp.

PART TWO

Great Fast Breads in Less Than Sixty Minutes

Great Fast Breads
in Less Than Sixty Minutes

Sweet Potato Biscuits

Even starting with a raw sweet potato, these delicious biscuits are ready to eat in less than one hour. If a boiled sweet potato happens to be in the refrigerator, however, the hot biscuits are ready to enjoy in just a bit over half an hour. Fill with some ham, and you have a match made in heaven.

Makes about fifteen 2-inch biscuits

> 1 medium sweet potato, about ½ pound
> 2 cups all-purpose flour
> 4 teaspoons baking powder
> 1 teaspoon salt
> ⅔ cup vegetable shortening, room temperature
> 2 or 3 tablespoons milk

Preheat oven to 400 degrees.

1. Cook the sweet potato until very soft, about 20 minutes. Peel and mash and put aside.

2. Sift the flour, baking powder, and salt into a mixing bowl. Add the shortening and cut it in with a pastry cutter or two knives. Since the shortening is soft, it will require a bit of pushing off the cutter. When the mixture is mealy, add the sweet potato and continue working with the pastry cutter.

3. Sprinkle 2 tablespoons of milk into the bowl and blend with a wooden spoon until the dough is soft and cohesive. Add the extra tablespoon of milk if necessary.

4. Pat the dough into a circle about ½-inch thick. Cut into 2-inch circles and place on an ungreased baking sheet. Bake 15 or 20 minutes or until the biscuits are puffy, a little darker in color, and feel firm. Serve warm.

Sour Cream Rolls

These light, buttery rolls have a texture very similar to that of brioche but are remarkably easy to make. They are best eaten warm so, if made ahead, wrap them in aluminum foil and reheat in a 350-degree oven for about three minutes.

Makes about eighteen 2-inch rolls

> 1 package proofable fast-rising yeast (2 teaspoons)
> *(see yeast note, page 5)*
> 3 tablespoons sugar, plus ¼ teaspoon
> pinch of nutmeg
> ¼ cup milk, heated to warm
> ½ cup butter, softened
> 3 eggs
> ½ teaspoon salt
> ½ cup sour cream
> 3 cups all-purpose flour

1. Stir the yeast, ¼ teaspoon sugar, and the nutmeg together in a cup. Pour in the milk, stir, and put aside in a warm spot. Cream together the butter and 3 tablespoons sugar. Add 2 eggs, one at a time, beating well after each addition. Stir in the salt and sour cream and blend them well into the mixture. Add the foamy yeast and stir again.

2. Put the flour in another bowl, make a well in the center, and pour the liquid mixture into the well. With a wooden spoon, work the flour into the liquid, beginning near the

center of the bowl, then making wider circles. Once all the flour is incorporated, beat well for 1 minute. Gather the dough into a ball, cover the bowl, and let the dough rest for 5 minutes.

Preheat oven to 350 degrees.

3. Grease a muffin tin or use paper-lined foil cups. Break off a piece of dough about the size of a golf ball, roll into a round between your palms, drop into one of the muffin cups, and press a little. Continue forming rolls with the rest of the dough. Cover the muffin tin with plastic wrap and place in a warm spot for about 20 minutes or until the dough fills the cups.

4. Beat the remaining egg and brush it over the tops of the rolls. Bake for 15 to 20 minutes or until the rolls are a deep golden brown and well puffed. Remove the tin from the oven, let the rolls stand for 5 minutes, then remove them from the cups. Serve warm.

Buttery Dinner Rolls

These yeast rolls receive only one rise but still have a wonderfully light texture. Since salt and too much sugar retard yeast growth they are added after the rise, which helps the enthusiastic puff.

Makes about eighteen rolls

> 1 package proofable fast-rising yeast (2 teaspoons)
> *(see yeast note, page 5)*
> pinch of ginger
> ¼ cup sugar
> 1½ cups warm water
> ½ cup dried skimmed milk
> 2½ cups bread flour
> 1 egg, room temperature, beaten
> 4 tablespoons butter
> ½ teaspoon salt

1. Put the yeast into a mixing bowl with the ginger and ¼ teaspoon of the sugar. Add the warm water and stir to dissolve the yeast, then add the dried milk. Add 2 cups of flour, half a cup at a time, while beating with a wire whisk. Beat vigorously until the batter becomes elastic and a lazy bubble erupts when the beating is stopped. Add the remaining half-cup flour and stir in with a wooden spoon. Add the egg and beat it into the batter. Cover the bowl and place in a warm spot for 30 minutes.

Preheat oven to 425 degrees.

2. While the batter is rising, melt the butter and liberally grease the muffin tins with oil or butter or prepare a sufficient number of paper-lined foil cups.

3. Sprinkle the salt and the rest of the sugar over the soft batter and beat with a wooden spoon to incorporate them thoroughly. Finally, add the melted butter and stir just until it is absorbed by the dough. The dough will be soft and elastic.

4. Spoon the batter into the prepared muffin tins, easing it off the spoon with a rubber spatula. Pour water into any unfilled muffin cups. Bake for about 15 minutes or until the rolls are golden brown on top and well puffed. Cool the rolls for 5 minutes, then remove them from the tins and serve warm.

Buttermilk Pan Rolls
(Food Processor)

This versatile dough can be used for rolls of many shapes. Baked in an 8-inch-square pan it produces jumbo hamburger buns. Daintier dinner rolls or hot dog buns emerge when baked in a rectangular baking dish measuring approximately 8 × 14 × 2 inches. The procedure and old-fashioned flavor are the same; only the ultimate use is different.

Makes nine to twenty-four rolls

> 1 package proofable fast-rising yeast (2 teaspoons)
>   *(see yeast note, page 5)*
> 2 tablespoons sugar
> pinch of ginger
> ¼ cup warm water
> 1 cup buttermilk
> ¼ cup vegetable shortening
> about 3 cups all-purpose flour
> ½ teaspoon baking soda
> 1 teaspoon salt
> 1 egg, beaten

1. Sprinkle yeast, ½ teaspoon sugar, and ginger into a small bowl. Pour in the warm water, stir to dissolve the yeast, and put aside in a warm place. Put half-cup buttermilk and shortening in a small pot over low heat until the shortening melts; remove from heat and stir in remaining buttermilk.

Liberally grease the baking dish, either a square pan or rectangular baking dish.

2. Measure 3 cups of flour, the baking soda, salt, and remaining 1¾ tablespoons sugar directly into the food processor and pulse a few times to aerate the flour. Add the buttermilk to the yeast and stir. With the motor running add the liquid mixture and process until a ball is formed. Feel the dough. If it seems very sticky add another ¼ cup of flour and process another 10 to 15 seconds.

3. Scrape the dough into the prepared baking pan, sprinkle flour over the surface, and press down with your hands to push the dough into an even layer. If necessary, dust lightly again with flour. Use a floured knife to cut the dough into the roll shape you desire. Cut almost, but not entirely, to the bottom of the pan. Wring out a cloth with hot water, drape over the pan, and place in a warm spot for 20 minutes.

Preheat oven to 400 degrees.

4. With a floured knife once again cut through the rolls to reemphasize the separations. Brush the top with the beaten egg and bake for about 20 minutes or until the rolls are puffed and golden brown. Remove the pan to a rack and cool for 15 minutes, then turn out the rolls, cool them on the rack, and pull apart.

Cottage Cheese Muffins

These little cupcakes have an agreeably moist interior because of the creamy cottage cheese. A touch of spiciness
makes them especially enjoyable as a snack or with fruit
salads.

Makes sixteen 2½-inch muffins

> ¼ cup butter, room temperature
> ⅔ cup dark brown sugar
> 1 lemon
> 2 eggs, beaten
> ¼ teaspoon ginger
> ¼ teaspoon nutmeg
> 1 tablespoon rum
> 1½ cups creamed cottage cheese
> ½ teaspoon salt
> ½ teaspoon baking soda
> 1½ cups all-purpose flour

Preheat oven to 350 degrees.

1. Arrange paper-lined foil muffin cups on a baking sheet
or thoroughly grease a muffin tin and four extra ovenproof
custard cups. In a mixing bowl cream together the butter and
sugar. Grate the rind of the lemon directly into the bowl; be
careful not to include any of the bitter white pith. Stir in the
eggs, ginger, nutmeg, and rum.

2. Either sieve the cottage cheese or mash thoroughly until the curds are small and add it to the creamed mixture. Sprinkle on the salt and baking soda and mix, then finally blend in the flour.

3. Fill the muffin cups two-thirds full and bake for about 30 minutes or until they are well puffed and golden; a toothpick plunged into the center should emerge dry.

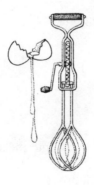

Cheese Muffins

There is no reason in the world one can't use a fresh piece of cheese for these delightful muffins. But thrifty souls might feel more inclined to use the odd bits and ends left over from cheese that has dried a little. Blue-veined cheeses make an especially interesting muffin.

Makes ten to twelve muffins

 2 cups all-purpose flour
 2 teaspoons baking powder
 2 tablespoons sugar
 ½ teaspoon salt
 ½ teaspoon paprika
 ½ teaspoon thyme
 2 eggs
 ½ cup milk
 ¼ cup butter, melted
 about ½ cup cheese cut into pieces

Preheat oven to 375 degrees.

1. Sift together into a mixing bowl the flour, baking powder, sugar, and salt. Add the paprika and thyme and stir briefly.

2. In a small bowl beat together the eggs, milk, and melted butter and pour over the dry ingredients. Stir the batter just until all the ingredients are blended; do not overmix or the muffins will be tough.

3. Grease a muffin tin or place paper-lined foil cups on a baking sheet. Spoon about a heaping tablespoon of batter into each cup, drop in a piece of cheese, and cover with another tablespoon of batter. Bake for about 25 minutes or until the muffins have puffed a little and are a nice golden brown. Cool the muffins in the tins for 5 minutes, then remove to a rack.

Maple-Nut Oatmeal Muffins

The combination of grains used in these muffins creates a nice mix of textures. They are delightful treats in the lunch box or in the breakfast bread basket.

Makes about twenty muffins

> 1 cup quick oatmeal
> 1½ cups buttermilk
> ½ cup pure maple syrup
> 1 cup whole wheat flour
> 1 cup cornmeal, white or yellow
> ½ teaspoon baking soda
> ½ teaspoon salt
> ½ cup walnuts or pecans, chopped

Preheat oven to 350 degrees.

1. Stir together in a mixing bowl the oatmeal, buttermilk, and maple syrup. Put aside for 5 minutes. Meanwhile, either grease muffin tins or arrange paper-lined foil cups on a baking sheet.

2. Sift onto the oatmeal mixture the whole wheat flour, cornmeal, baking soda, and salt. Stir only until the ingredients are well blended, then add the nuts and stir briefly again. Spoon the batter into the muffin tins and bake for about 25 minutes. Cool the muffins for 5 minutes before removing from the tins onto a rack.

Irish Soda Bread

There is controversy among soda bread traditionalists. Some contend that Irish Soda Bread must be baked in a deep, covered pot so it can steam a little before being uncovered to finish baking with a crisp crust. Others say that's too fussy for such a homespun bread, especially since the covered pot is a hangover from when breads were baked over open fires and a small oven had to be created. I tend to agree with the topless theory.

Makes one round loaf (1¼ pounds)

> 3 cups all-purpose flour
> 1 teaspoon salt
> ½ tablespoon baking soda
> 1 tablespoon sugar
> 3 tablespoons lard (2 tablespoons melted)
> about 1⅓ cups buttermilk, room temperature

Preheat oven to 375 degrees.

1. Place all the dry ingredients—the flour, salt, baking soda, and sugar—in a large mixing bowl. Stir the melted lard into 1⅓ cups buttermilk and put the remaining tablespoon of lard in a heavy 9- or 10-inch cast-iron skillet and place it in the oven. Pour the buttermilk into the bowl and stir with a fork; if the batter seems too dry, add another tablespoon or two of buttermilk.

2. Flour a pastry board, pull the dough onto it, and knead for 2 or 3 minutes. Pat the dough into an 8-inch round. Very carefully remove the hot skillet from the oven and place the round of dough in it. Use a small, sharp, floured knife to cut a deep cross into the top of the dough. Place in the oven and bake for about 30 minutes or until the top is nicely browned and crisp. Use a sturdy spatula or heavy pot holders to turn the bread out onto a rack to cool. Cool for about 30 minutes and break apart into quarters. This bread should be sliced thin. It keeps very well.

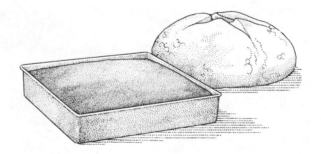

Brown Irish Soda Bread

The preceding recipe discusses the arguments for using different baking utensils for Irish Soda Bread. Just to prove that it really doesn't matter, this loaf is baked on a baking sheet. Whole wheat flour gives soda bread a deeper flavor.

Makes one 8-inch round (1¼ pounds)

> 2 cups whole wheat flour
> 1 cup all-purpose flour
> ½ tablespoon baking soda
> ½ teaspoon salt
> 1 cup buttermilk

Preheat oven to 375 degrees.

1. Measure the flours, baking soda, and salt into a mixing bowl. Add the buttermilk and stir with a fork until the mixture is well blended. Pull the dough onto a floured board and knead for a minute or two, then pat into an 8-inch round.

2. Grease a sturdy baking sheet and place the round of dough on it. Use a sharp, floured knife to cut a deep cross into the top of the bread; this allows more even distribution of heat. Bake for about 40 minutes or until the loaf is well browned and crisp. Cool on a rack.

Corn Breads

Cornmeal breads come down to us with the most colorful names in the bread lexicon. Often the title reflects the early American's practical streak, so we have Hoecakes because they were baked on a hoe and Spoonbread because that's how the bread is taken from its baking dish. There are some names that are mistranslations of Indian words, such as Corn Pone instead of *apone*. However the name came about, the breads are delicious and crisp and usually are eaten hot. Here are a few, even an Italian version.

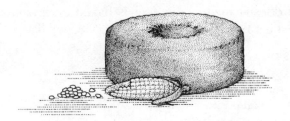

Spoon Bread

This is one cornmeal bread name that needs no great explanation—it is served with a spoon because its consistency is that of a thick pudding. As with most traditional recipes, there are many versions. My favorite is the one served at Christiana Campbell's Tavern in historic Williamsburg, Virginia. They are so proud of it that they hand out copies of the recipe. This is it, but since I can't leave anything alone, you will find some minor changes.

Makes eight servings

1⅓ cups water
1 cup yellow cornmeal
2 teaspoons sugar
1½ teaspoons salt
4 tablespoons butter, cut into pieces
1⅓ cups milk
3 eggs
1 tablespoon baking powder

Preheat oven to 350 degrees.

1. Grease a 6-cup soufflé dish and put aside. Put the water on to boil while measuring into a mixing bowl the cornmeal, sugar, and salt. As soon as the water reaches a full boil, pour it into the bowl, add the butter, and stir until the mixture is thick and the butter is melted.

2. Stir in half the milk. Beat the eggs until light and add them to the bowl, beating the batter very well. Finally, put the baking powder in a 2- or 3-cup mixing bowl, then slowly add the remaining milk while stirring the mixture into a thin paste. This combination will froth impressively, graphically demonstrating the leavening quality of baking powder; oven heat releases still more leavening. Add the foaming milk to the batter and mix well.

3. Scrape the batter into the greased dish and place it in a larger pan. Pour in enough hot water to reach halfway up the sides of the soufflé dish. Bake for about 45 minutes or until the top is nicely puffed and browned and a knife plunged into the center emerges moist but with no batter clinging to it. Remove from the oven, allow the dish to remain in the water bath for 5 minutes, then serve. The bread is scooped out of the dish with a large spoon.

Souffléd Corn Bread

Because of the beaten egg white leavening, this corn bread has a lighter and smoother texture than most. In fact, the technique for combining the beaten whites with the stiff batter is precisely the same as for a true soufflé. A word about beating egg whites: I have found that when working with a relatively small amount, a rotary hand beater is ideal, that is, if you're not using a copper bowl and whisk. A hand-held electric beater is too fast, even at its lowest speed. A good rotary beater, preferably one with gears, turns out super-thick and velvety beaten whites.

Makes one 5-inch round bread (about 1 pound)

> ¼ pound butter (1 stick)
> 1 cup yellow cornmeal
> ¼ cup sugar
> ½ teaspoon salt
> 3 eggs, room temperature
> pinch of cream of tartar

Preheat oven to 375 degrees.

1. Cut the butter into large pieces and melt; put aside to cool. Select a 5-inch mold such as a charlotte pan or a soufflé dish and cut a piece of wax paper to fit the bottom. Butter the mold liberally, place the paper in it, and butter the paper.

2. Pour the cornmeal, sugar, and salt into a mixing bowl and stir with a wooden spoon. Separate the eggs, dropping

the yolks into a small bowl and the whites into a bowl large enough for beating.

3. While beating the yolks with a whisk or fork, slowly pour in the cooled melted butter. Pour this mixture over the dry ingredients in a slow, steady stream while stirring with a wooden spoon. Beat well for a minute to blend all the ingredients thoroughly and completely moisten the cornmeal. It will be a very stiff mixture.

4. Beat the egg whites for a few seconds until they begin to froth, add the cream of tartar, and beat the whites until they are thick and firm but not dry. Scoop about one-third of the whites over the cornmeal batter and thoroughly blend them into the batter to lighten it. Give a few extra strokes to the remainder of the beaten whites, scrape them over the batter, and gently fold them in. Do not overmix; it is far better to leave a few visible bubbles of white than to break them down.

5. Scrape the batter into the prepared mold and bake about 30 minutes or until the top is lightly browned and the bread begins to pull away from the sides of the mold. A toothpick plunged into the center should come out clean. Cool about 5 minutes in the mold, turn out, remove the wax paper, and serve immediately or cool on a rack.

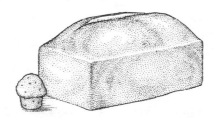

Spider Corncake

Why spider? Because the original baking utensil used for this quick bread was a cast-iron skillet with legs, not as many legs as a spider, but enough to give it the unusual name. That practical early American pan could be set over coals in the fireplace with enough elevation to accomplish baking instead of frying. There are many versions of this custardy bread. Some use white cornmeal, others insist on yellow; molasses is called for at times, but so is sugar. I prefer a mixture of molasses and sugar to give a softer molasses flavor and color.

Makes one 10-inch bread (2 pounds)

>   2 tablespoons lard or butter
>   1½ cups cornmeal, white or yellow
>   ½ cup all-purpose flour
>   1 tablespoon sugar
>   ½ teaspoon salt
>   1 teaspoon baking soda
>   2 eggs
>   1 tablespoon unsulfured molasses
>   1 cup buttermilk
>   2 cups milk

Preheat oven to 350 degrees.

1. Put the lard in a 10-inch cast-iron skillet and place in the hot oven while preparing the batter. Measure the cornmeal, flour, sugar, salt, and baking soda into a mixing bowl and stir

to blend the ingredients. In another bowl beat together the eggs, molasses, buttermilk, and 1 cup of the milk and pour over the dry ingredients. Stir the batter just until the liquid and dry ingredients are thoroughly blended.

2. Using several thicknesses of pot holders, remove the skillet from the oven and rotate it so the melted lard coats the sides as well as the bottom. Pour the batter into the hot skillet. Slowly pour the remaining 1 cup of milk over the surface. Do not sitr and do not be alarmed that the milk does not remain on the surface; it will sink into the thin batter and create a slightly custardy interior. Bake for about 30 minutes or until the top is puffed and the sides begin pulling away from the skillet. Cut into wedges and serve hot.

Chili Corn Bread

One of the pleasures of baking with cornmeal is its versatility. It has a distinctive flavor but also can be an accommodating vehicle for more emphatic additions. Here is one excellent example of the latter role.

Makes one 10-inch round bread (1½ pounds)

    1 cup yellow cornmeal
    1 teaspoon baking soda
    ¼ teaspoon ground pepper
    ¼ pound Monterey Jack cheese, grated
    2 eggs
    ½ cup buttermilk
    1 cup canned cream-style corn
    4 tablespoons bacon fat or lard, melted
    2 to 3 tablespoons chopped hot green chili peppers, or to
    taste

Preheat oven to 375 degrees.

1. Oil a 10-inch cast-iron skillet and place it in the oven to heat. In a mixing bowl stir together cornmeal, baking soda, and pepper. Toss in the cheese and mix to coat the cheese with cornmeal.

2. Push the cornmeal away from one side of the bowl and break in the eggs. Beat them lightly with a wooden spoon, then stir into the cornmeal. Add the buttermilk, corn, and melted fat and mix well. Finally, stir in the chili peppers.

3. Using several heavy pot holders, remove the skillet from the oven, scrape in the batter, and bake for about 35 minutes or until the bread begins to pull away from the sides of the skillet and a knife plunged into the center comes out dry. Serve hot from the skillet, cutting the bread into wedges.

Cornmeal Bread with Onions and Garlic (Pane di Granoturco con Cipolle e Aglio)

The flavorings added to this Italian country corn bread can be varied to suit your mood or the dish it will accompany. This is the combination I like, but you might prefer cheddar cheese instead of Parmesan and some herbs. For the adventurous I would like to point out that some versions augment the onion, garlic, and cheese with raisins and nuts—a combination that puzzles me.

Makes one 10-inch round bread

> ¼ cup olive oil
> 1 medium onion, chopped fine
> 1 garlic clove, minced
> 2½ cups hot water
> 1 teaspoon salt
> ½ teaspoon pepper
> 2 cups yellow cornmeal
> ½ cup Parmesan cheese, grated

Preheat oven to 350 degrees.

1. Select a heavy 9- or 10-inch cast-iron skillet, pour in the olive oil, onion, and garlic and fry until soft, about 5 minutes. Remove the skillet from the heat and add the hot water, salt, and pepper. Return the skillet to the fire and bring the water

to a boil, then slowly pour in the cornmeal, stirring constantly. Keep stirring until the mixture thickens. Remove from the heat, stir in the cheese, and smooth the top with a rubber spatula. (If preferred, the batter can be poured into a greased oblong baking dish.)

2. Bake the bread for about 25 minutes or until the surface is dry and lightly colored and the sides begin pulling away from the skillet. Using plenty of pot holders, remove the skillet from the oven, cool for 5 minutes, and cut into wedges.

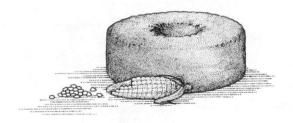

About Zucchini Breads

Zucchini is one of the mildest squashes in the garden. For this reason it lends itself to an endless parade of preparations in the kitchen. In bread-making its role is mostly visual and textural, but that is an important role. Recipes in other parts of the book and those for the two following breads contain zucchini that has been grated and sweated. Please do not believe any bread recipe that does not specify ridding the vegetable of its liquid. The author either assumed you know that it should be done or the recipe never went through a kitchen. If the shreds are not divested of all their moisture (and zucchini is 95 percent water), the baked loaf will be waterlogged.

The usual method for drawing out the moisture is to salt the shreds liberally and allow them to wilt for at least half an hour, then rinse and squeeze. For the purposes of this book, I suggest another method that eliminates the salt and the waiting time: simply freeze the grated zucchini. Defrosting automatically separates the vegetable's moisture from the solid. Of course, this means advance preparation so that the zucchini is available when the mood strikes you to bake a green-flecked loaf. I like to shred several pounds at a time and freeze them in one-pound batches. It is a great way to take care of the late-summer squash glut. Defrosting can be accomplished at room temperature in an hour or so or speeded up by immersing the frozen bag in very warm water. I usually dump the frozen shreds into a colander and run hot water over them for half a minute. No matter what method you use, squeeze out all the liquid a handful at a time.

Chips' Zucchini Bread

The chipper woman (hence for nickname) for whom this bread is named is a dedicated cook and baker. She is famous for this zucchini bread, which I've adapted to make it less sweet and faster to prepare. She assures me that the results are as good—if not so dessertlike. See the note about frozen zucchini on page 64.

Makes one loaf (1¼ pounds)

> 1 pound zucchini, grated, frozen, and thawed
> 2 eggs
> ½ cup oil
> ½ cup sugar
> 1½ cups all-purpose flour
> ½ teaspoon salt
> ½ teaspoon baking soda
> ⅛ teaspoon baking powder
> 1 teaspoon cinnamon
> ½ cup raisins
> ½ cup nuts, chopped

Preheat oven to 350 degrees.

1. A handful at a time, squeeze all the water from the defrosted grated zucchini. In a mixing bowl beat together the eggs, oil, and sugar. Add the flour, salt, baking soda, baking powder, and cinnamon and beat well to blend the dry and liquid ingredients thoroughly. Fold in the zucchini, then the raisins, and finally the nuts.

2. Cut a piece of wax paper to fit the bottom of a loaf pan. Grease the pan, lay in the wax paper strip, and grease it as well. Scrape in the batter and bake for about 40 minutes or until a toothpick plunged into the center comes out clean. Cool in the pan for 5 minutes, then turn out, remove the wax paper, and place on a rack to cool.

Zucchini Corn Bread

This version of zucchini bread has an emphatic herby flavor that marries well with hearty soups and stews. The addition of grated cheese adds both a piquant note and an orangey hue to play against the green of the vegetable. See the note about frozen zucchini on page 64.

Makes one loaf (1½ pounds)

> 4 tablespoons butter
> 2 ounces sharp cheddar cheese
> 1 pound zucchini, grated, frozen, and thawed
> 1 cup all-purpose flour
> ¾ cup yellow cornmeal
> 1 tablespoon baking powder
> 1 teaspoon salt
> 2 tablespoons dried onion soup
> ½ teaspoon celery seed
> ½ teaspoon thyme
> 1 egg
> 1 cup buttermilk

Preheat oven to 400 degrees.

1. Melt the butter in a small pot and set aside to cool. Grate the cheese and set aside; there should be about ½ cup. A handful at a time, squeeze all the water from the defrosted grated zucchini.

2. In a large mixing bowl combine the flour, cornmeal, baking powder, salt, dried onion soup, celery seed, and thyme and stir to blend all the ingredients.

3. Break the egg into a small bowl and beat lightly, then pour in the buttermilk and the melted butter. Pour this liquid mixture over the dry ingredients and beat vigorously to combine them thoroughly. Stir in the zucchini and the grated cheese.

4. Cut a piece of parchment or wax paper to fit the bottom of a loaf pan. Grease the pan, lay in the paper strip, and grease the paper. Scrape in the batter and bake for about 35 minutes or until a toothpick plunged into the center comes out clean. Cool in the pan for 5 minutes, then turn out, remove the paper strip, and place on a rack to cool.

Olive Bread

This exotic bread has an intriguing blend of flavors. Pungent olives are balanced by dots of cheese, while the ham adds a slightly smokey taste and a very pretty color. Olive bread is especially compatible with luncheon and brunch menus or with white wine on a warm afternoon.

Makes one loaf (about 1½ pounds)

> 2¼ cups all-purpose flour
> 4 eggs
> ½ cup olive oil
> ⅓ cup white wine
> 1 teaspoon baking powder
> ¼ pound gruyere or Swiss cheese in 1 slice, cut into tiny dice
> ¼ pound ham in 1 slice, cut into tiny dice
> ½ cup black olives, preferably oil-cured or Mediterranean style, cut into small pieces
> ½ cup green olives, cut into small pieces

Preheat oven to 375 degrees.

1. Put the flour in a large mixing bowl and make a well in the center. Beat the eggs and oil together and pour into the well. In a small bowl stir the wine into the baking powder to dissolve it, then add this, too, to the liquid ingredients in the bowl. Slowly incorporate the flour into the liquid ingredients and beat well for several minutes. Add the cheese, ham, and olives and mix again.

2. Oil a loaf pan, place a piece of parchment or wax paper in the bottom, and oil the paper. Scrape the batter, which will be quite thick, into the pan. Bake for 10 minutes, then reduce the heat to 350 degrees and bake another 30 to 35 minutes or until a toothpick plunged into the center comes out clean. Cool the loaf slightly before turning out and removing the paper. Cool on a rack.

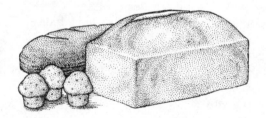

Onion-Topped Bread

Onion is often used as an unexpected flavoring inside breads, such as the yeast loaf on page 120. Not so here. An emphatic quantity of this pungent member of the lily family is strewn right on top and baked into a golden layer. This savory bread is baked in a dish and meant to be eaten hot. It is excellent with meat roasts.

Makes one 12 × 8 × 2-inch bread

> 1½ pounds onions (about 5 or 6)
> ¼ cup butter
> 2 cups all-purpose flour
> 1 tablespoon baking powder
> 1 teaspoon salt
> 1 teaspoon sugar
> ½ teaspoon caraway seeds
> 3 eggs
> 1½ cups milk
> 1 cup sour cream
> pepper to taste

Preheat oven to 375 degrees.

1. Slice the onions thin and sauté in butter in a covered skillet for about 5 minutes. Do not allow the onions to brown; cook just until they are limp. Scrape them into a bowl. Grease a baking dish measuring approximately 12 × 8 × 2 inches.

2. Sift the flour, baking powder, salt, and sugar into a mixing bowl. Stir in the caraway seeds. Beat together in a small bowl 1 egg and the milk and pour over the dry ingredients. Stir the batter with a fork just until all the ingredients are blended; do not overmix. Scrape the batter, which will be a little thin, into the prepared dish and smooth into an even layer with a spatula.

3. Use the same small bowl for beating together the remaining 2 eggs and the sour cream and season with pepper. Add this mixture to the onions and stir well to blend the onions and the enrichment. Spread the onions over the top of the batter, scattering them into an even layer with a fork. Bake for about 30 minutes or until the custardy topping has set and a sharp knife plunged into the bread layer comes out dry. If you prefer a deeper color on top, slip the dish under the broiler for half a minute. Cool for 5 minutes, then cut into squares and serve.

Bacon-Cheese Bread

The success of this loaf depends largely on the quality of the olive oil. It must be a strong virgin oil that is capable of imparting its character to the bread. Fry a few extra slices of bacon some morning and keep refrigerated until you are inspired to make bread. This batter receives no preliminary rise, which accounts for its loose texture.

Makes one loaf (1¾ pounds)

> 1 teaspoon proofable fast-rising yeast
> *(see yeast note, page 5)*
> ¼ teaspoon sugar
> pinch of ginger
> ¼ cup warm water
> ¼ pound sharp cheddar cheese
> 4 or 5 slices bacon, fried crisp
> 2½ cups all-purpose flour
> 4 eggs
> ¾ cup virgin olive oil
> ½ cup dry vermouth

Preheat oven to 350 degrees.

1. Sprinkle the yeast into a small bowl, add the sugar and ginger, and stir in the water. Put aside in a warm spot for 5 minutes. Meanwhile, cut the cheese into tiny cubes and crumble the bacon. Grease a loaf pan, fit a piece of parchment or wax paper into the pan, and grease it as well.

2. Put the flour in a mixing bowl, add the eggs and olive oil, and beat for 1 minute. Add the yeast and vermouth and beat another 5 minutes. Stir the cheese and bacon into the batter and mix briefly.

3. Pour the batter into the prepared pan and bake for 15 minutes. Reduce the heat to 300 degrees and bake for another 30 to 35 minutes or until a toothpick plunged into the center comes out clean. Cool for 5 minutes before turning out and removing the paper.

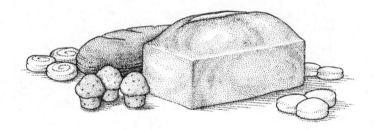

Pizza Bread (with or without food processor)

Making pizza at home is almost faster than going out for it. Since the bread base is the foundation of pizza, it is included in this book. A list of suggested toppings follows, but they only hint at the possibilities.

Makes one 12- to 14-inch pizza

> 2 cups all-purpose flour
> 1 package fast-rising yeast (2 teaspoons)
> *(see yeast note, page 5)*
> ¼ teaspoon salt
> ¾ cup water
> 1 tablespoon olive oil

1. Put the flour, yeast, and salt in the container of a food processor and pulse a few times to aerate the flour. Meanwhile, heat the water to 130 degrees or use very hot tap water, add the olive oil, and pour into the processor with the motor running. Stop the motor when the mixture forms a ball. Oil a mixing bowl, drop the dough into it, cover, and place in a warm spot to rise for 30 minutes. (If you do not have a food processor, incorporate the ingredients in a bowl in the order listed above. Add the 130-degree water and olive oil and stir with a wooden spoon until the dough begins to take shape, then continue kneading by hand until the dough is smooth, about 10 minutes.)

Preheat oven to 450 degrees.

2. Pull the dough onto a floured board, knead the dough for 1 minute, and shape into a ball.

3. Oil a pizza pan, place the dough on it, and, with oiled hands, spread the dough to cover the surface of the pan. A 12-inch pan will have a baked crust almost half an inch thick; a 14-inch pan will have a thin crust. Top with any desired ingredients and bake for 10 minutes or until the crust is crisp and the topping is piping hot. Serve at once by cutting into wedges.

Suggested Pizza Toppings:

Tomato Sauce and Mozzarella Cheese

Tomato Sauce with Fried Onions, Mushrooms, and Mozzarella Cheese

Tomato Sauce with Sliced Sausage, Sautéed Green Peppers, and Parmesan Cheese

Tuna Fish Mixed with Ricotta Cheese and Capers

Grated Cheddar Cheese mixed with Sautéed Red and Green Peppers and sprinkled with Olive Oil

Clam Sauce and Parmesan Cheese

Any others you can think of

Fried Bread

Frying dough, especially sweet dough, is a very popular cooking procedure all over Europe. It probably was created when hungry children wanted a quick snack and mother had a batch of bread dough lazily rising. A different look and taste can be achieved by topping with sesame and poppy seeds before frying.

Makes fourteen 4-inch rounds

> 1 package proofable fast-rising yeast (2 teaspoons)
>   *(see yeast note, page 5)*
> ¼ teaspoon sugar
> pinch of nutmeg
> about 1 cup warm water
> about 4 cups all-purpose flour
> ½ teaspoon salt
> lard or oil for frying
> Optional: about ½ cup sesame or poppy seeds

1. In a mixing bowl stir 1 teaspoon of the yeast, the sugar, and nutmeg with ¼ cup of warm water. Put aside in a warm spot for 5 minutes. Add the remaining ¾ cup of warm water and ½ cup flour, cover, and let rise in a warm spot for 15 minutes.

2. Sprinkle the remaining teaspoon of dry yeast over the sponge and stir. Add the salt and the rest of the flour and beat well. Add a few tablespoons of warm water if the dough

seems too dry. Turn the dough onto a board and knead until a smooth, soft ball is formed, about 10 minutes. Add extra flour if necessary. Put the bowl over the dough and let rest for another 10 minutes.

3. Pull off a piece of dough about the size of a large egg and flatten it into a round about 4 inches in diameter. If using the seeds, sprinkle about a teaspoon over the top and press it with the palm of your hand. When 3 or 4 of the rounds are ready put ½ cup of lard or oil in a wide skillet. When the fat is medium hot slip in the dough rounds, seeded side up, and fry over medium heat until golden brown underneath, about 5 minutes. Turn and fry the other side the same way. Transfer the fried breads to a baking sheet lined with paper towels. Continue shaping and frying the rest of the dough, adding more fat as needed. Serve hot.

Note: If the bread is fried in advance, reheat in a 400-degree oven for about 5 minutes. The fried bread rounds can also be frozen and reheated without defrosting for 10 minutes in a 400-degree oven.

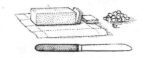

Fried Indian Flatbread

American Indian cooking includes several versions of fried breads. Some begin with cutting fat, usually lard, into the flour, much as in biscuit making. Others are simply stirred together, as is this one. The bread is simplicity itself to prepare, but the resulting fried round has a lavish look—golden brown, crackling crisp, and replete with airy pockets. If you have a helper, even a child, to do the rolling, the whole recipe can be done in less than thirty minutes.

Makes eight 8-inch rounds

>   2½ cups all-purpose flour
>   1½ tablespoons baking powder
>   1 teaspoon salt
>   1 tablespoon dried skimmed milk
>   ¾ cup warm water
>   1 tablespoon vegetable oil
>   oil for frying

1. In a mixing bowl stir together the flour, baking power, and salt. Pour the dried milk into a small bowl, add the water and vegetable oil, and stir to dissolve the milk. Pour this liquid over the dry ingredients and stir until a smooth dough evolves; this should take only a minute or two. If the dough seems too soft, sprinkle in another tablespoon of flour. Knead the dough in the bowl for half a minute. Cover with a cloth and let the dough rest for 10 minutes.

2. Meanwhile, select a large skillet, at least 10 inches wide, and pour in oil to a depth of about 1 inch. Begin to heat the oil very slowly. Also line a baking sheet with paper towels and place near the skillet.

3. Divide the dough into eight sections, take one piece of dough, and keep the rest covered in the bowl. Roll the dough into a ball and flatten with your hand, then roll into a very thin circle 8 to 10 inches across. Thinness is the key to the puffy results. Make a hole in the center with your finger or use the end of the handle of a wooden spoon. Very lightly dust the top of the disk, put aside, and cover with a cloth. Continue with the rest of the dough in the same manner.

4. As you begin to roll the last piece of dough, turn up the heat under the skillet to bring the oil up to 375 degrees. Slip a circle of dough into the hot oil and fry for about 1 minute or until the bottom is golden brown. Turn with tongs or a wide perforated spatula and fry the other side for another minute. Remove the fried bread to the prepared baking sheet and continue with the rest of the bread rounds.

5. Fried Indian Flatbread is best eaten hot and crisp. When cooled, it can be placed in plastic bags and frozen; freshen without defrosting by placing on a baking sheet for 5 minutes in a 400-degree oven.

Russian Onion Flatbread (Non)

On a recent trip to Soviet Central Asia I marveled at the variety of plain and decorative breads sold in the farmers' markets in Tashkent and Samarkand. Many bakers seemed to compete to produce the most fanciful version. These were mostly flatbreads, some with a little leavening, others with none. High-standing loaves for slicing were sold only in government stores. It was also served in restaurants, but we invariably brought our own flatbread from the market. This is but one thin, crisp example.

Makes about sixteen 8-inch rounds

1½ cups onions, minced
6 tablespoons butter
¾ cup warm water
1½ teaspoons salt
2½ to 3 cups all-purpose flour

1. In a covered skillet fry the onions in 1 tablespoon of butter for about 5 minutes and set aside. Melt the remaining 5 tablespoons of butter and pour into a mixing bowl. Add the water, salt, and onions. A half-cupful at a time, stir in 2½ cups of flour, or just enough to produce a dough that is soft but not sticky. Gather the dough into a ball on a pastry board, cover with the bowl, and let rest for 10 minutes.

2. Divide the dough into sixteen balls, each about 1½ inches in diameter, and roll out on a lightly floured board

into a circle 7 to 8 inches wide. When there are seven or eight rolled-out rounds, begin frying them while continuing to roll the remainder.

3. Select a heavy 10- to 12-inch skillet and place over high heat without any grease. When it is hot enough to make a drop of water bounce briskly, place a circle of dough on it and fry for about 2 minutes or until the bottom is dry and flecked with dark spots. Turn the flatbread over with your fingers or a wide spatula, fry for another minute or so, and transfer to a rack. Scrape out any bits of onion that may have stuck to the skillet. Continue frying the remaining rounds.

4. These flatbreads are at their best eaten warm but can always be rewarmed in a slow oven. Store them loosely covered so they will retain their crispness. If they become limp, dry them out in a 250-degree oven for about 5 minutes.

Caraway Flatbread

Caraway seeds and rye bread are indelibly linked in the world of breads. This simple flatbread proves how much flavor and interest the little crescent-shaped seeds can bring to plain old all-purpose flour.

Makes one 9-inch round flatbread (1 pound)

> 1½ cups all-purpose flour
> 2 teaspoons baking power
> 2 tablespoons sugar
> ¼ teaspoon salt
> 3 tablespoons cold butter, diced
> 3 tablespoons cold lard, diced
> 1 tablespoon caraway seeds
> 2 eggs
> ½ cup milk

Preheat oven to 350 degrees.

1. Oil a 9-inch pie dish. Sift the flour, baking powder, sugar, and salt directly into a mixing bowl and stir briefly with a wooden spoon. Add the butter and lard and work into tiny bits with a pastry cutter or two knives until the mixture resembles a coarse grain. Sprinkle in the caraway seeds.

2. Beat the eggs in a small bowl, stir in the milk, and pour over the dry ingredients. Mix together with the wooden spoon just until the batter is blended; do not overmix.

3. Scrape the stiff batter into the prepared pie dish and smooth into an even layer with a rubber spatula. Bang the dish on the counter once or twice to settle the batter well into the dish. Bake for about 25 minutes or until the bread is puffy on top and the sides begin to pull away from the dish; a toothpick inserted into the center should come out clean. Cut into wedges. Caraway Flatbread can be served warm or completely cooled.

Note: For freezing, cut the round into four wedges and wrap tightly.

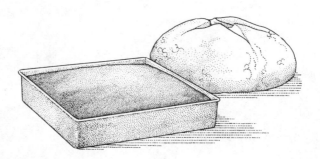

Whole Wheat Deep-Dish Bread

This yeast bread is not a flatbread or a puffed loaf. It is a delicious maverick of something in between. The batter is baked in a deep pie dish and produces only a modest puff.

Makes one 10-inch bread (1 ¾ pounds)

> 2 packages proofable fast-rising yeast (4 teaspoons)
>   *(see yeast note, page 5)*
> ½ teaspoon sugar
> ¼ teaspoon nutmeg
> ½ cup warm water
> 1 cup milk
> 2 tablespoons honey
> ¼ teaspoon fennel seeds
> 2 eggs
> ¼ cup oil
> 1 teaspoon salt
> 1½ cups whole wheat flour
> 1½ cups cornmeal, yellow or white

Preheat oven to 325 degrees.

1. In a small bowl stir together the yeast, sugar, and nutmeg. Stir in the warm water and put aside in a warm spot. Meanwhile, heat the milk in a small pot with the honey and fennel, just enough to melt the honey. Cool to lukewarm. While waiting for the milk, liberally butter a deep 10-inch pie dish.

2. Break the eggs into a mixing bowl, add the oil, and beat together with a wire whisk. Scrape in the frothy yeast and stir. Slowly add the warm milk while whisking rapidly. Finally, stir in the salt, whole wheat flour, and cornmeal. Beat thoroughly with a wooden spoon to blend all the ingredients. The batter will be fairly stiff. Scrape the batter into the prepared pie dish and bake for about 35 minutes or until puffed, brown, and a toothpick plunged into the center comes out clean. Cut the bread into wedges while still warm.

Irish Oatmeal Flatbread

Oatmeal and buttermilk are combined in several recipes on these pages. In this one, however, they are put together in a different manner, and the result is a denser texture.

Makes one 7-inch flatbread (¾ pound)

> 1¼ cups buttermilk
> 2 cups quick oatmeal
> 1¼ cups all-purpose flour
> ½ teaspoon baking soda
> ¼ teaspoon mace
> 1 teaspoon salt

Preheat oven to 375 degrees.

1. Put the buttermilk in a small pot and bring to the boiling point. Meanwhile, pulverize the oatmeal in a blender or food processor and pour into a large mixing bowl. Pour the hot buttermilk over the oatmeal, stir briefly, cover, and put aside for 5 minutes.

2. Add the flour, baking soda, mace, and salt and mix into a soft dough. Knead the dough in the bowl for about 3 minutes. Grease a heavy baking sheet, gather the dough into a ball, and place on the sheet. Pat the dough into a round about 1 inch thick and 7 or 8 inches in diameter.

3. Flour a sharp knife and cut the round into quarters; the pieces will be separate, but do not push them apart. Bake for about 30 minutes or until the bread takes on a dark tan color and a sharp knife plunged into the center comes out clean.

Bread Sticks (Grissini)

Watch any group of diners in an Italian restaurant. What is the first thing they reach for? *Grissini*, those thin, crisp bread sticks that generally sprout from tall glasses. The snap and crackle of the long, dry rolls is part of the traditional sound effects of an Italian meal. But you don't have to be Italian to enjoy them or to make them. Moreover, homebaked *grissini* can be produced with a variety of flavorings. Most recipes for bread sticks say to roll out the dough and cut it into strips. I prefer to roll pieces of dough between the palms to produce a rounder—if less uniform—stick. Remember, if the sticks aren't razor straight it proves they did not come out of a box.

Makes about twenty-six 8-inch bread sticks

2 cups all-purpose flour
1 package fast-rising yeast (2 teaspoons)
   (see yeast note, page 5)
1 teaspoon salt
¾ cup water
1 tablespoon mild olive oil or plain vegetable oil
Optional: 1 egg white beaten with 1 teaspoon water; coarse
salt; or poppy, fennel, sesame, or caraway seeds

1. Put the flour, yeast, and salt into the container of a food processor and pulse a few times to aerate the flour. Meanwhile, heat the water to 130 degrees or use very hot tap water, add the olive oil, and pour into the processor with the

motor running. Stop the water when the mixture forms a ball.

2. Pull the dough onto a floured board, knead the dough for 1 minute, and shape into a ball. Oil a mixing bowl, drop the dough into it, cover, and place in a warm spot to rise for 30 minutes. (If you do not have a food processor, incorporate the ingredients in the bowl in the order listed above. Add the 130-degree water and olive oil and stir with a wooden spoon until the dough begins to take shape, then continue kneading by hand until the dough is smooth, about 10 minutes.)

Preheat oven to 450 degrees.

3. Grease a baking sheet. Pull off a piece of dough about the size of a large walnut and roll it between your palms until it is about 8 inches long and pencil thin. Place it on the baking sheet and continue with the rest of the dough. Do not work in a warm area at this time because the intent is to prevent a second rise, which would produce an airy texture rather than a firm, crisp interior. Place the sticks about an inch apart to allow for expansion.

4. Depending on preference, you can bake the *grissini* Italian-style—without any garnishing—or brush with the egg white wash and sprinkle with any of the suggested garnishes. Bake for 8 to 10 minutes or until they are nicely browned and crisp. Remove the bread sticks from the baking sheet at once and cool on a rack. They keep extremely well, several weeks in fact, but not in an air tight container.

Armenian Seed Crackers

These crisp cracker breads make a very showy display on the buffet table, be it brunch, lunch, or dinner. They are not bland crackers that require a spread; they are well-seeded and stand out on their own.

Makes twelve 8-inch rounds

> 2 ¾ cups all-purpose flour
> 1½ tablespoons poppy seeds
> 1 tablespoon fennel seeds
> 1 tablespoon caraway seeds
> 1 tablespoon sugar
> 1 teaspoon salt
> 1 egg
> 2 tablespoons lard, melted
> ⅔ cup water

1. Put the flour, all the seeds, sugar, and salt into a mixing bowl. Beat the egg and lard in a small bowl, then add the water. Pour the liquid mixture over the dry ingredients and rapidly stir together with a fork. Knead the dough into a ball, cover with plastic wrap, and put in the freezer for 15 minutes.

Preheat oven to 375 degrees.

2. Oil several baking sheets. Cut the dough into twelve sections and put them on a dish covered with plastic wrap. On

a floured board roll out one section at a time into a circle 7 to 8 inches in diameter and transfer to the baking sheet.

3. Bake the cracker breads for 10 minutes, turn, and bake 3 to 5 minutes more or until they are crisp and lightly browned in spots. Cool on a rack.

Note: The dough can be prepared in a food processor using the same procedure as above, pouring in the liquid mixture with the motor running.

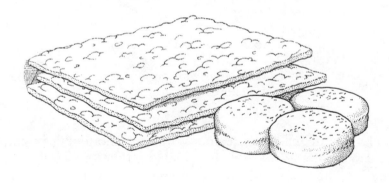

Oatmeal Crisps

Even though these small crisps have a mild flavor, they can become addictive. Somewhere between English oatcakes and Scandinavian flatbread, Oatmeal Crisps are delicious from breakfast to service with cheese at dinner.

Makes about forty-two crisps

> 2 tablespoons vegetable shortening, room temperature
> 1 tablespoon butter, room temperature
> 2 tablespoons sugar
> ¼ teaspoon salt
> ¼ teaspoon ground coriander
> ¼ teaspoon baking soda
> ½ cup rolled oats, regular or quick-cooking
> about 1¼ cups all-purpose flour
> ½ cup buttermilk

1. In a mixing bowl cream together the shortening, butter, and sugar until very smooth. Sprinkle on the salt, coriander, and baking soda and cream another half-minute. Add the rolled oats and blend in thoroughly. Add 1 cup of the flour and the buttermilk alternately to make a stiff dough. If necessary, add the remaining ¼ cup of flour, a tablespoon at a time. The dough may remain somewhat sticky. Scrape the dough onto a sheet of wax paper about 20 inches long and pat it into a rectangle. Fold the wax paper over the dough and put in the freezer for 15 minutes.

Preheat oven to 325 degrees.

2. Put a piece of aluminum foil, about 20 inches long, on a work surface, dull side up. Open up the wax paper covering the dough and put the dough in the center of the aluminum foil with the wax paper over it. Roll the dough between the foil and the wax paper until very thin. The wax paper permits you to see the shape and thickness of the dough. Try to make as even a rectangle as possible. Lift the dough with the foil and wax paper onto a cookie sheet, foil side down. Carefully peel off the wax paper and discard.

3. With a floured knife cut the dough into squares, diamonds, long, thin strips, or 2 × 3-inch rectangles. Do not drag the knife, but lift it and make successive cuts. Place in the oven for about 20 minutes or until the thinner outer edges are a light brown and the crisps feel firm. Cool on the cookie sheet, then break apart and store in an airtight container. They will keep indefinitely.

Apple Coffee Cake

This excellent coffee cake loaf can be enriched by the addition of walnuts, pecans, or macadamias. The cake is best, of course, when fresh, but it also refrigerates and freezes very well. It is a handy loaf to have waiting in the freezer for sudden needs.

Makes one loaf (1½ pounds)

> 2 or 3 tart apples (about ½ pound)
> 8 tablespoons butter
> 2 eggs
> ⅔ cup sugar
> 2 tablespoons buttermilk
> 1 teaspoon vanilla
> ½ teaspoon cinnamon
> ¼ teaspoon nutmeg
> ¼ teaspoon salt
> 2 teaspoons baking powder
> ½ teaspoon baking soda
> 2 cups all-purpose flour

Preheat oven to 350 degrees.

1. Liberally grease a loaf pan, fit a piece of wax or parchment paper in the bottom, and grease the paper. Peel, quarter, core, and grate the apples. Melt the butter in a heavy skillet and add the apples, turning them over and over to coat the fruit thoroughly with the butter. Simmer for 30 seconds, take off the heat at once and set aside.

2. Beat together the eggs and sugar, then add the buttermilk, vanilla, cinnamon, nutmeg, salt, baking powder, and baking soda. Mix all ingredients together very well. Add the flour slowly and beat it in thoroughly. The batter will be very stiff but will lighten as the apples and melted butter are stirred in.

3. Pour the batter into the prepared loaf pan and bake for about 45 minutes or until the top surface cracks and a toothpick plunged into the center comes out clean. Allow the loaf to cool in the pan for 10 minutes, then remove to a rack.

Lemon Loaf

A treat any time—as a breakfast bread, with a luncheon salad, during a coffee break, or in the dinner bread basket. The lemon scent is fresh and delicate and utterly captivating.

Makes one loaf (1 pound)

>   ½ cup butter, softened
>   ½ cup sugar
>   2 eggs
>   1 lemon
>   ½ teaspoon ground coriander
>   1½ cups all-purpose flour
>   2 teaspoons baking powder
>   ½ teaspoon salt
>   ½ cup milk

Preheat oven to 350 degrees.

1. Oil a loaf pan, fit a piece of wax or parchment paper in the bottom, and oil it as well. Use a wire whisk to cream the butter while slowly adding the sugar. Beat until the mixture is light and fluffy; the more air mixed into the batter base the better. Add the eggs, one at a time, whisking well between each addition.

2. Grate the rind of the lemon directly into the bowl, then squeeze the juice of the lemon and add to the creamed mixture. Sprinkle in the coriander and stir. The mixture will look slightly curdled, but it does not matter.

3. Measure the flour, baking powder, and salt into a sifter and sift them into the bowl one-third at a time, alternating with the milk. Thoroughly incorporate each addition before continuing. Beat the batter for about half a minute, then scrape into the prepared loaf pan. Bake for about 45 minutes or until the top is brown and puffed with a small crack in the center; a toothpick plunged into the center should emerge dry. Cool for 10 minutes in the pan before removing.

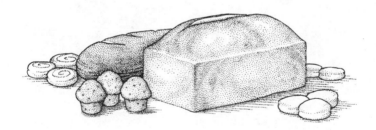

Cinnamon Coffee Cake

A cup of steaming coffee or tea tastes even better when enjoyed with a piece of Cinnamon Coffee Cake. This sweetened
bread is child's play to put together and proves again that
quality is not always measured by complexity.

Makes one 8 × 10 × 2-inch sweet bread

> 1½ cups all-purpose flour
> ⅔ cup sugar
> 2 teaspoons baking powder
> ½ teaspoon baking soda
> ½ teaspoon salt
> 2 eggs
> 1 cup sour cream

> TOPPING:
> 1 tablespoon sugar
> 2 teaspoons cinnamon
> ⅛ teaspoon nutmeg
> 1 tablespoon butter

Preheat oven to 350 degrees.

1. Sift together the flour, sugar, baking power, baking
soda, and salt. In a small bowl beat together the eggs and
sour cream and stir into the dry ingredients. Beat the batter
well.

2. Spread the batter into a greased 8 × 10 × 2-inch baking dish and bake for about 30 minutes or until a toothpick plunged into the center comes out dry.

3. While the cake is baking, mix together the tablespoon of sugar, cinnamon, and nutmeg. Immediately upon removing the cake from the oven, rub the butter over the hot surface and sprinkle with the flavored sugar. Return the pan to the oven for 1 minute, then cool.

Ice-Cream Bread Loaf

This loaf begins just like Ice-Cream Muffins (page 23); only the baking mold is different. Because the loaf takes longer to bake it is included here. To give the bread a different character, raisins or chopped dates can be added. I find this loaf is best baked in a straight-sided ovenproof glass dish.

Make one 8 × 4 × 2½-inch loaf (1¼ pounds)

> 1 pint vanilla ice cream
> 1 egg
> 2 tablespoons oil
> 1½ cups all-purpose flour
> 1 tablespoon baking powder
> 1 teaspoon salt
> Optional: ½ cup raisins or chopped dates

Preheat oven to 425 degrees.

1. Cut a piece of parchment or wax paper to fit the bottom of an ovenproof glass loaf dish. Oil the dish, lay the paper in, move it around a little, then flip it over.

2. Prepare the batter according to the directions for Ice-Cream Muffins (page 23), adding the raisins or dates at the end if desired. Pour the batter into the loaf dish. Bake for 25 to 30 minutes or until golden brown on top and a toothpick plunged into the center comes out clean. Place the dish on a rack, let cool for 10 minutes, then remove the paper. Cool on the rack.

Blueberry Loaf

This colorful fruit loaf can be a two-fer. First, enjoy it for its own good self, then if there are any leftovers, slice, cover with a mixture of sour cream and brown sugar, broil, and present as dessert.

Makes one loaf (1½ pounds)

> 2 cups all-purpose flour
> ⅔ cup sugar
> 1 tablespoon baking powder
> ¼ teaspoon nutmeg
> ½ teaspoon salt
> 1 cup blueberries
> 3 eggs
> ⅔ cup milk
> ¼ teaspoon almond extract
> ½ cup butter, melted

Preheat oven to 375 degrees.

1. Grease a loaf pan, fit a piece of wax paper in the bottom, and grease it. Sift the flour, sugar, baking power, nutmeg, and salt into a large mixing bowl. Add the blueberries and stir lightly to coat the berries with flour. If using frozen berries, partially defrost them.

2. In a small bowl beat together the eggs, milk, almond extract, and butter; pour over the contents in the bowl and stir

briefly with a fork, just until the liquid and dry ingredients are blended.

3. Scrape the batter into the prepared pan, bang on the counter to settle the batter well into the pan, and smooth the top with a moistened spatula. Place in the oven and bake for about 40 minutes or until the top is puffed, nicely browned, and cracked. Remove to a rack and cool for at least 15 minutes before turning out of the pan. This loaf slices best when completely cooled.

PART THREE

Great Fast Breads
in Less Than Ninety Minutes

Great Fast Breads
in Less Than Ninety Minutes

Beer Bread

This rough-textured loaf keeps extremely well and is especially good toasted. The beeriness of its flavor depends, naturally, on the kind of beer used—less heavy types produce a milder-tasting bread.

Makes one loaf (1½ pounds)

> 3½ cups all-purpose flour
> ¼ cup sugar
> 1½ cups beer, room temperature
> 1 egg, room temperature
> 2½ tablespoons oil

Preheat oven to 375 degrees.

1. Grease a loaf pan. Measure the flour and sugar into a mixing bowl and stir to blend them. Pour the beer into a 2-cup measure, add the egg and 2 tablespoons of oil, and beat all together briefly with a fork. Add the liquid ingredients to the bowl and stir to blend them thoroughly, but do not beat or overmix.

2. Scrape the batter into the prepared pan and bake for 15 minutes. Brush the remaining ½ tablespoon of oil over the top of the loaf and return to the oven for another 45 minutes or until a toothpick plunged into the center comes out moist but with no batter clinging to it. Remove the bread from the pan and cool on a rack.

No-Knead, No-Rise Buttermilk Bread

This remarkable loaf of bread defies logic. Instead of kneading, it receives a scant five minutes of beating in the bowl,
which, incidentally, eliminates the onerous chore of cleaning
a crusty board. Furthermore, the dough is put into the oven
without any rising and still bakes into a beautiful loaf. You
will find two major departures from most bread recipes: the
dough is very wet and the pan goes into a cold oven. What
began as an accident, my friends now call magic.

Makes one loaf (1¼ pounds)

> ½ cup buttermilk
> 2½ tablespoons butter, cut into pieces
> 2 tablespoons sugar, plus ¼ teaspoon
> 1 teaspoon salt
> 1 teaspoon proofable fast-rising yeast
> *(see yeast note, page 5)*
> pinch of ginger
> ¼ cup warm water
> ⅔ cup cold water
> 3 cups all-purpose flour
> ¼ teaspoon vinegar
> ½ tablespoon butter, melted

1. In a small pot over medium fire heat together the buttermilk, butter, 2 tablespoons of sugar, and the salt. Stir a few
times until the butter has melted and pour into a large mixing bowl. Proof the yeast while the buttermilk is heating: stir

together in a small bowl the yeast, ginger, and remaining ¼ teaspoon of sugar. Pour in ¼ cup warm water, stir, and put aside for a few minutes until frothy.

2. To the hot buttermilk in the bowl add ⅔ cup cold, not icy, water and stir in 1 cup of flour. Add the vinegar to the yeast and blend into the batter. Beat well.

3. Add the remaining 2 cups of flour and beat vigorously with a wooden spoon for 5 minutes. The batter will be stiff and a little sticky; don't be alarmed. Under the rough treatment of the beating the dough becomes creamy looking and somewhat cohesive. Incidentally, I find sitting down the most comfortable position for this procedure.

4. Oil a loaf pan and scrape the batter in. It will be stubborn and not slide out of the bowl easily. Bang the pan on the counter a few times and smooth the top with a rubber spatula dipped in cold water.

5. Place the pan in a cold oven, turn on the heat to 325 degrees, and bake for 30 minutes. Brush the top of the loaf with the melted butter and return to the oven for another 45 minutes or until the loaf sounds hollow when rapped on the bottom. Cool on a rack.

No-Knead, No-Rise Zucchini Bread

Zucchini is most often used in baking powder breads. It works just as well in more substantial yeast breads. With less than fifteen minutes working time, any cook can turn out this attractive and tasty loaf.

Makes one loaf (1½ pounds)

1 pound frozen zucchini *(see note, page 64)*
½ cup buttermilk
2½ tablespoons butter, cut into pieces
2 tablespoons sugar, plus ¼ teaspoon
1 teaspoon salt
1 teaspoon proofable fast-rising yeast
   (see yeast note, page 5)
½ teaspoon nutmeg
¼ cup warm water
⅔ cup cold water
3 cups all-purpose flour
1 teaspoon ground coriander
¼ teaspoon vinegar
¼ cup cornmeal
½ tablespoon butter, melted

1. Put the zucchini in a colander and defrost under running hot water. A handful at a time, squeeze out as much water as possible, then put the shreds in a bowl and fluff them.

2. In a small pot over medium fire, heat together the buttermilk, butter, 2 tablespoons of sugar, and the salt. Stir a few times until the butter has melted and pour into a large mixing bowl.

3. Proof the yeast while the buttermilk is heating: stir together in a small bowl the yeast, ¼ teaspoon nutmeg, and the remaining ¼ teaspoon of sugar. Pour in the warm water, stir, and put aside for a few minutes until frothy.

4. To the hot buttermilk in the bowl, add the cold, not icy, water, and stir in 1 cup of flour, the coriander, and ¼ teaspoon nutmeg. Add the vinegar to the yeast and blend it into the batter. Beat well.

5. Add the remaining 2 cups of flour and beat vigorously with a wooden spoon for 5 minutes. The batter will be stiff and a little sticky but will become creamy under the heavy beating. Sitting down is usually the most comfortable position for this step. After about 3 minutes of beating, toss the zucchini with the cornmeal to coat it and add to the batter. Continue beating for 2 more minutes.

6. Oil a loaf pan and scrape the dough in. It will be stubborn and not slide out of the bowl easily. Bang the pan on the counter a few times and smooth the top with a rubber spatula dipped in cold water.

7. Place the pan in a cold oven, turn on the heat to 325 degrees, and bake for 30 minutes. Brush the top of the loaf with the melted butter and return to the oven for about another 45 minutes or until the loaf sounds hollow when rapped on the bottom. Cool on a rack.

No-Knead, No-Rise Whole Wheat Bread I

This is another bread that requires no kneading or rising, and the resulting loaf is no less successful for its ease. Whole wheat flour is a little heavier to work with than other flours, so a sturdy arm is needed for the beating. Remember, though, five minutes of vigorous beating is still far better than the usual fifteen minutes of hard kneading.

Makes one loaf (1½ pounds)

½ cup buttermilk
3 tablespoons butter, cut into pieces
3 tablespoons sugar, plus ¼ teaspoon
1 teaspoon salt
1 package proofable fast-rising yeast (2 teaspoons)
    (see yeast note, page 5)
pinch of ginger
¼ cup warm water
¾ cup cold water
1½ cups bread flour
¼ teaspoon vinegar
1½ cups whole wheat flour
beaten egg

1. In a small pot over a medium fire heat together the buttermilk, butter, 3 tablespoons of sugar, and the salt. Stir a few times until the butter has melted and pour into a large mix-

ing bowl. While the buttermilk is heating, proof the yeast: stir together in a small bowl the yeast, ginger, and remaining ¼ teaspoon of sugar. Pour in ¼ cup warm water, stir, and put aside for a few minutes until frothy.

2. To the hot buttermilk in the bowl add ¾ cup cold, not icy, water and stir in 1 cup of the bread flour. Add the vinegar to the yeast and blend into the batter. Beat well.

3. Add the remaining half-cup of bread flour and the whole wheat flour and beat vigorously for 5 minutes with a sturdy wooden spoon. The dough will change its appearance during the beating and become more cohesive but still will seem a little shaggy; it will never look as smooth and satiny as regular bread doughs. Let the dough rest in the bowl for 5 minutes.

4. Oil a loaf pan and scrape the batter in. It will be stubborn and not slide out of the bowl easily. Tap the pan on the counter a few times and smooth the top with a rubber spatula dipped in cold water.

5. Place the pan in a cold oven, turn on the heat to 325 degrees, and bake for 30 minutes. Brush the top with the beaten egg and return to the oven for another 40 minutes. Remove the loaf from the pan and place in the oven for 5 minutes or until it sounds hollow when rapped on the bottom. Cool on a rack.

No-Knead, No-Rise Whole Wheat Bread II

At first glance it may seem strange to have two similar recipes for the same kind of bread. There is a good reason. The preceding recipe for No-Knead, No-Rise Whole Wheat Bread calls for bread flour and buttermilk, two items that may not be on hand when you feel an urge to make whole wheat bread. Adjustments have been made in the recipe to accommodate more ordinary ingredients.

Makes one loaf (1½ pounds)

> ½ cup milk
> 2 tablespoons sugar, plus ¼ teaspoon
> 3 tablespoons butter, cut into pieces
> 1 package proofable fast-rising yeast (2 teaspoons)
>   *(see yeast note, page 5)*
> large pinch nutmeg
> ½ cup warm water
> ⅔ cup cold water
> 1½ cups all-purpose flour
> ½ teaspoon vinegar
> 1½ cups whole wheat flour
> 1 teaspoon salt

1. Put the milk, 2 tablespoons sugar, and the butter in a small pot and heat over medium fire until the butter melts. Meanwhile, mix the yeast with the nutmeg and remaining ¼

teaspoon sugar and stir in the warm water. Put aside in a warm spot. Grease a loaf pan.

2. Pour the hot milk into a large mixing bowl and add the cold water and 1 cup all-purpose flour. Use a wire whisk to blend all the ingredients. Add the vinegar to the foamy yeast and scrape it into the bowl, then whisk vigorously for about 1 minute. Add the remaining ½ cup all-purpose flour and all the whole wheat flour and beat with a wooden spoon for 5 minutes. The batter will be stiff and sticky but under the heavy beating will acquire a smooth appearance. Add the salt and beat an additional minute, then scrape the batter into the prepared pan. Bang the pan on the counter a few times and smooth the top with a wet rubber spatula.

3. Place the pan in a cold oven, turn on the heat to 325 degrees, and bake for about 1 hour and 15 minutes or until the loaf sounds hollow when rapped on the bottom. Cool on a rack.

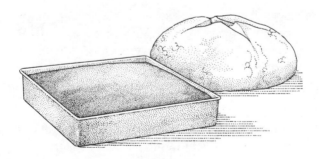

Sandwich Bread I (Food Processor)

Because of the close texture of this loaf it cuts into neat, even slices—perfect for sandwiches. The crust is firm but not brittle.

Makes one loaf (1 pound)

> 1 teaspoon proofable fast-rising yeast
> *(see yeast note, page 5)*
> 1 tablespoon sugar, plus ¼ teaspoon
> pinch of ginger
> 1 cup warm water
> about 2½ cups bread flour
> ½ teaspoon salt
> ¼ teaspoon vinegar

1. Sprinkle the yeast, ¼ teaspoon sugar, and ginger into a 2-cup measuring cup, add ¼ cup warm water, and stir to dissolve the yeast. Put aside in a warm spot. Meanwhile, oil a deep mixing bowl and measure 2¼ cups of flour into the food processor with 1 tablespoon of sugar and the salt. Strike the pulse switch a few times to aerate the flour a little.

2. Add the remaining ¾ cup warm water to the yeast along with the vinegar. With the motor running pour in the liquid mixture and, once the dough forms a ball, process for another 10 or 15 seconds. Feel the dough; if it is sticky sprinkle on a little more flour and process again briefly. On a lightly floured board knead the dough about ten times. Drop the

ball of dough into the prepared bowl and flip it around a few times to coat with oil. Cover the bowl with plastic wrap and place in a warm spot to rise for 25 minutes.

Preheat oven to 425 degrees.

3. While the dough is rising oil a loaf pan. Punch down the dough, knead briefly, and transfer to the loaf pan. Cover with plastic wrap and place in a warm spot for another 30 minutes. (If you are pressed for time, give the dough only a 20-minute rise; the results will be almost as good.)

4. Remove the plastic wrap and bake the loaf for 10 minutes; reduce the heat to 350 degrees and bake another 20 minutes. Turn out the loaf and rap the bottom; if it sounds hollow the bread is ready, if not, return to the oven for another 5 minutes. Remove the loaf from the pan and cool on a rack.

Sandwich Bread II (Food Processor)

This is a variation of the preceding recipe but does not call for proofing of the yeast.

Makes one loaf (1 pound)

> about 2½ cups bread flour
> 1 teaspoon fast-rising yeast
> ½ teaspoon salt
> 1 tablespoon sugar
> pinch ginger
> 1 cup water
> ¼ teaspoon vinegar

1. Measure directly into the food processor the flour, yeast, salt, sugar, and ginger and pulsate a few times to mix the ingredients and aerate the flour. Heat the water to 125 to 130 degrees, add the vinegar, and pour into the processor with the motor running. Once the dough forms a ball, process for another 10 to 15 seconds. Feel the dough; if it is sticky sprinkle on a little more flour and process again briefly.

2. On a lightly floured board knead the dough about ten times. Generously oil a mixing bowl, drop the dough into it and flip it around a few times to coat the ball with oil. Cover the bowl with plastic wrap and place in a warm spot to rise for 30 minutes.

Preheat oven to 425 degrees.

3. While the dough is rising oil a loaf pan. Punch down the dough, knead briefly, and transfer to the loaf pan. Cover with the plastic wrap and place in a warm spot for another 30 minutes.

4. Remove the plastic film and bake the loaf for 10 minutes; reduce the heat to 350 degrees and bake another 20 minutes. Turn out the loaf and rap the bottom; if it sounds hollow the bread is ready, if not return to the oven for another 5 minutes. Remove the loaf from the pan and cool on a rack.

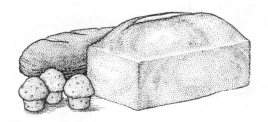

French Loaves (Food Processor)

A food processor removes the heavy-duty kneading necessary to turn out airy French bread. It also reduces the time required to produce the long, crusty loaves and make the recipe eligible for this ninety-minute section. To make a similar bread without the machine see Long French Loaves (page 178).

Makes two 16-inch loaves (½ pound each)

3½ cups bread or all-purpose flour
1 package fast-rising yeast (2 teaspoons)
    (see yeast note, page 5)
½ teaspoon sugar
pinch of ginger
1⅓ cups water
1 teaspoon salt

1. Measure the flour, yeast, sugar, and ginger directly into the food processor and pulse 2 or 3 times. Heat the water to between 125 and 130 degrees and, with the motor running, pour the hot water into the machine, then immediately add the salt. Process until the dough forms a ball and allow the machine to run for another half a minute to knead it. Pull the dough onto a lightly floured board, knead for 1 minute, and gather into a ball.

2. Grease a mixing bowl and drop the dough into it, flip the dough to coat it with fat, cover with a cloth soaked in hot

water and wrung out, and put aside to rise in a warm spot for 30 minutes. Meanwhile, thoroughly grease *baguette* pans—long, fluted loaf pans—reaching all the way to the top. If you do not have these pans, grease a sturdy baking sheet.

Preheat oven to 400 degrees.

3. Turn the dough onto a clean board with no flour on it and knead just ten times. Gather the dough into a ball and cut in half. Roll the dough against the board to make a rope about 15 inches long and 2 inches in diameter. Place the rope in the pans or on the sheet. Repeat with the other half of dough. Cover with plastic wrap and place in a warm spot for about 20 minutes.

4. Slash each loaf in four or five places with a very sharp knife or a razor. Do not make deep slashes, but make them at a shallow 45-degree angle. Brush the surface of the loaves with ice water or oil. Ice water will help create steam in the oven and give the loaves a crisp but dull crust. I prefer to brush with oil for a golden, shiny crust. Bake for 15 minutes, reduce the temperature to 350 degrees, turn the pan around, and continue baking for another 20 to 30 minutes or until the bottom of the loaf sounds hollow when rapped. Remove from the pans at once and cool on a rack. If the loaves seem to be getting too dark during the baking, cover loosely with aluminum foil.

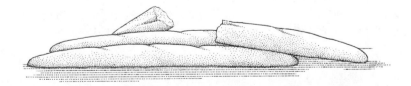

Onion Bread

Good onion bread does not reek of onion, it just lets you
know it's there. This excellent loaf can be a snack in itself.
Try toasting it, topping with a slice of cheese, and broiling
just until the cheese melts.

Makes one loaf (1½ pounds)

> 1 package proofable fast-rising yeast (2 teaspoons)
> *(see yeast note, page 5)*
> 2 tablespoons of sugar, plus ¼ teaspoon
> large pinch of ginger
> 2 cups warm water
> 3 tablespoons shortening
> about 4 cups all-purpose flour
> ⅓ cup onion, minced
> 1 teaspoon salt
> 2 eggs, beaten

1. In a small bowl stir the yeast, ¼ teaspoon sugar, ginger,
and 1 cup warm water; put aside in a warm spot. Meanwhile,
melt the shortening in the remaining cup of water over medium heat. Put 2 cups of flour in a large mixing bowl and
add the remaining 2 tablespoons of sugar and the onion.

2. Pour the hot water and shortening over the flour and
beat well with a wooden spoon until the temperature is reduced to 115 degrees. Stir in the yeast and beat vigorously
for 2 minutes. Add another cup of flour, the salt, and most of

the eggs, reserving about 1 tablespoon for glazing. Beat for another minute.

3. On a well-floured board knead the dough for about 5 minutes, adding just enough additional flour to produce a firm dough that is not sticky. Grease a bowl, drop in the dough, cover with a cloth soaked in hot water and wrung out, and put aside in a warm spot for 15 minutes.

Preheat oven to 375 degrees.

4. Grease a loaf pan. Punch down the dough, turn out onto a floured board, and roll, or preferably pat into a rectangle approximately 14 × 7 inches. Lift one of the shorter sides and roll the dough up tightly, pressing well with each turn. Pinch the ends and the seam and place in the prepared pan, seam side down. Cover with plastic wrap and put aside in a warm spot for 20 minutes.

5. Brush the loaf with the reserved beaten egg and bake for about 35 minutes or until the loaf is well browned and sounds hollow when rapped on the bottom. Remove from the pan and cool on a rack.

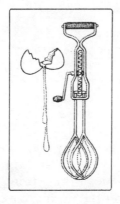

Raisin-Cinnamon Bread

Either cream cheese or jelly (or both together) makes an ideal spread for this delicious bread. But try it with gruyere cheese for a delightful change-of-pace combination. When turned into hot toast and smeared with butter it will brighten any breakfast.

Makes one loaf (1½ pounds)

> 1 teaspoon proofable fast-rising yeast
>   *(see yeast note, page 5)*
> 2 tablespoon sugar, plus ¼ teaspoon
> pinch of nutmeg
> ¼ cup warm water
> 3 tablespoons rum
> ½ cup raisins
> ½ cup milk
> 1 cup quick-cooking oatmeal
> 2 eggs, room temperature, beaten
> ½ teaspoon salt
> ½ tablespoon cinnamon
> ⅛ teaspoon ground cardamom
> about 2½ cups all-purpose flour

1. Put the yeast, ¼ teaspoon sugar, and nutmeg in a large mixing bowl; pour in the water and stir to mix. Put the bowl aside in a warm spot. Meanwhile, bring the rum to the boiling point and pour over the raisins, cover and put aside. Heat the milk to lukewarm, no more than 115 degrees.

2. To the frothy yeast add the oatmeal and 2 tablespoons sugar, then stir in the milk and the rum drained from the raisins. Next add the eggs, salt, cinnamon, and cardamom. Mix well with a wooden spoon. Add 2 cups of the flour and beat until the dough pulls away from the bowl.

3. Put another half-cup of flour in a corner of a kneading board; liberally sprinkle some of this flour over the board and scrape the batter onto the board. Vigorously knead for 10 minutes, incorporating the rest of the flour. If the dough feels extremely soft, add just a bit more flour. Spread the dough out, add the raisins, and knead for another minute.

4. Grease a loaf pan and put the dough into it. Cover with a damp cloth and let rise for 30 minutes in a warm spot.

Preheat oven to 375 degrees.

5. Bake the bread for 35 minutes or until it sounds hollow when rapped on the bottom. Remove to a rack and cool.

Single-Rise Sandwich Bread

Since this dough is not as wet as that for the no-knead, no-rise breads, it is kneaded for ten minutes. It is given only one rise, but if the directions are followed precisely the finished loaf will have a texture and crumb indistinguishable from double-rise loaves.

Makes one loaf (1¼ pounds)

> 1 package proofable fast-rising yeast (2 teaspoons)
>   *(see yeast note, page 5)*
> 1 tablespoon sugar, plus ¼ teaspoon
> pinch of ginger
> 1¼ cups warm water
> ¼ cup dried skimmed milk
> 2 tablespoons oil
> about 3 cups flour, preferably bread, or all-purpose
> 1 teaspoon salt
> ½ tablespoon butter, melted

1. Sprinkle the yeast, ¼ teaspoon sugar, and the ginger into a large mixing bowl. Pour in ¼ cup warm water, stir, and put aside in a warm spot for a few minutes. Meanwhile, oil a loaf pan.

2. Add the remaining cup of water to the yeast as well as the dried milk, oil, 1 tablespoon sugar, and 1½ cups flour. Beat vigorously with a sturdy wooden spoon for about 1 minute or until you can see an occasional lazy bubble erupt

when you stop beating. Add another cup of flour and mix into a stiff dough.

3. Put about half a cup of flour in a small dish near the dough board. Lightly flour the board, turn the dough onto it, and begin kneading while adding more flour until the dough is smooth and elastic, about 10 minutes. Handle the dough roughly to build up as much gluten as possible. Pull and stretch and punch. When the dough begins to lose its stickiness and hints at becoming smooth, stretch it out and sprinkle with the salt and continue kneading. Gather the dough into a ball, lightly flour the board, and vigorously throw the dough against it sixty times. Pretend you are furious. Transfer the dough to the prepared pan and brush the top with the melted butter. Soak a cloth in hot water, wring out, and drape it over the pan. Place the pan in a warm spot for 30 minutes.

Preheat oven to 375 degrees.

4. Bake the bread for about 25 minutes or until the bottom sounds hollow when rapped. Remove the loaf from the pan and cool on a rack.

Top-Hat Bread

There are a number or breads baked in coffee cans that emerge as high-rising, puffed-up loaves. They are decorative as well as exceptional eating. I think you will find this an especially rewarding version since it has a beautifully airy interior surrounded by a dark brown crust that is not too brittle. More sugar can be added, but I find the bread more versatile with the measure given here.

Makes two loaves (¾ pound each)

> 1 package proofable fast-rising yeast (2 teaspoons)
>   *(see yeast note, page 5)*
> ¼ cup sugar, plus ¼ teaspoon
> large pinch of nutmeg
> ¼ cup warm water
> ½ cup milk
> ¼ cup cold water
> ½ cup oil
> 1 teaspoon salt
> about 4 cups all-purpose flour
> 2 eggs, room temperature, beaten
> Optional: 1 tablespoon heavy cream

1. Pour the yeast into a small bowl and add ¼ teaspoon sugar and the nutmeg. Add the warm water and stir to dissolve the yeast granules, then set aside in a warm spot. Meanwhile, cut two pieces of wax paper to fit the bottoms of two coffee cans or similarly shaped molds, such as a charlotte

mold. Grease the interior of the cans, place the paper rounds in the bottoms, then grease the paper.

2. Heat the milk in a saucepan until almost scalded; do not bring to a full boil. Pour the hot milk into a large mixing bowl and add the cold water, oil, ¼ cup sugar, and the salt. Add 1 cup of flour and mix well. Stir in the foamy yeast and the eggs and beat very vigorously for about 2 minutes. Add enough of the remaining flour to produce a stiff batter. Again beat the dough vigorously for about 3 minutes or until it becomes elastic and you see an occasional lazy bubble pop up when you stop beating.

3. Scrape the batter into the prepared cans and rap the molds sharply on the counter to settle the dough into the bottom. Either snap on the plastic lids of the coffee cans or cover with plastic wrap held in place with a rubber band. Place the cans in a warm spot for 30 minutes or until the dough rises to the three-quarter level. Do not allow the dough to rise to the top of the cans.

Preheat oven to 375 degrees.

4. Remove the lids from the cans, brush with the cream if a shiny top is desired, then bake for about 35 minutes or until the bread is well browned and puffed over the top of the can. Cool in the can for 10 minutes, then turn out, remove the wax paper, and place on a rack to cool completely. If you like a crisper crust, return the unmolded breads to the oven for 5 minutes, but turn off the heat.

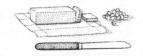

Sour Milk Bread

Yes, this recipe calls for sour milk, not buttermilk. Today's sour milk is a much more forceful product than the clabbered liquid mother used to salvage for pancakes. Milk is now ultrapasteurized, preventing it from souring naturally. It really is more spoiled than soured, but I found that it still makes a remarkably good, deeply flavored bread and just about the best toast imaginable.

Makes one loaf (1¼ pounds)

> 1 package proofable fast-rising yeast (2 teaspoons)
>   *(see yeast note, page 5)*
> 1 teaspoon sugar
> pinch of nutmeg
> ¼ cup warm water
> 2 tablespoons butter, melted
> 1 cup sour milk, room temperature
> 2 cups all-purpose flour
> 2 eggs, room temperature, lightly beaten

Preheat oven to 350 degrees.

1. In a large mixing bowl stir the yeast, sugar, and nutmeg together; add the water and put aside for 5 minutes in a warm place. Meanwhile, oil a loaf pan, fit a strip of wax paper in the bottom, and flip it over.

2. Add the butter and sour milk to the bowl, then thoroughly stir in the flour. Add the eggs and beat the batter for

3 minutes. Scrape the batter into the prepared pan—it will be soft—cover with a damp cloth and put in a warm spot for 15 minutes.

3. Bake the loaf for about 35 minutes or until well browned. Remove it to a rack to cool. The loaf may shrink a little as it cools.

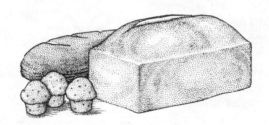

Dark Beer Bread

The beer is not dark, but the bread is—although it's lighter in color than pumpernickel. This interesting loaf receives an earthy taste from the beer; cocoa and a bit of molasses account for the depth of color.

Makes one loaf (1 pound)

> 1 teaspoon proofable fast-rising yeast.
> *(see yeast note, page 5)*
> ¼ teaspoon sugar
> pinch of nutmeg
> ¼ cup warm water
> 1 cup beer
> 2 tablespoons honey
> 2 teaspoons unsulphured molasses
> 2 tablespoons butter, cut in pieces
> 1 tablespoon cocoa
> 2¼ cups bread flour
> ½ teaspoon cinnamon
> ½ tablespoon fennel seeds

1. Mix the yeast, sugar, and nutmeg together in a small bowl; pour in the water and stir. Put aside in a warm spot. In a saucepan boil together for 1 minute the beer, honey, and molasses. Put the butter and cocoa in a large mixing bowl and pour the hot liquid over them, stirring until the butter melts. Add 1 cup of flour and test the temperature of the batter to make certain it does not exceed 115 degrees.

2. Scrape the foamy yeast into the bowl and beat with a wire whisk until smooth. Add the remaining flour, cinnamon, and fennel seeds and beat vigorously with a wooden spoon for 5 minutes. The batter will take on a lighter color and creamy quality but will remain soft and spongy. With an oiled spatula scrape the batter down into the bowl, cover with a damp cloth, and allow to rise in a warm spot for 30 minutes.

Preheat oven to 375 degrees.

3. Meanwhile, grease a loaf pan, fit a piece of wax or parchment paper in the bottom, and grease it as well. Beat the dough for a few seconds and scrape into the prepared pan. Smooth the top with a wet spatula, cover, and put aside to rise for 15 minutes in a warm spot.

4. Bake the loaf for about 30 minutes, remove from the pan, and place back in the oven for about another 5 minutes or until it sounds hollow when rapped on the bottom. Cool on a rack.

Bourbon Rolls

Real bourbon lovers would probably like a stronger flavor of
the golden liquid. Glazing the hot rolls with a thin frosting of
bourbon stirred into confectioners' sugar produces a flavor
to brighten the heart of any Kentucky lass or lad.

Makes about twenty-four 2-inch rolls

> 1 package proofable fast-rising yeast (2 teaspoons)
>   *(see yeast note, page 5)*
> ⅓ cup sugar, plus ¼ teaspoon
> large pinch of nutmeg
> ¼ cup warm water
> 2 cups milk
> about 3½ cups all-purpose flour
> ¼ pound butter (1 stick), room temperature
> 2 eggs, room temperature
> ⅓ cup bourbon

1. Stir the yeast, ¼ teaspoon sugar, and the nutmeg together in a small bowl. Add the warm water, stir, and put
aside in a warm spot. Scald 1 cup of milk. Sift 1½ cups of the
flour into a large mixing bowl, add the remaining cup of cold
milk, and stir. Then add the hot milk and stir again. Beat for
1 minute. Add the foamy yeast and beat well with whisk for
about 2 minutes. Cover with plastic wrap and let rise in a
warm spot for 30 minutes.

Preheat oven to 450 degrees.

2. After about 20 minutes of rising time cream the butter until it is soft and creamy. Gradually add the remaining ⅓ cup sugar, then, one at a time, add the eggs. Beat with a wire whisk for a minute. Sift the remaining 2 cups of flour into the creamed base, alternating with ¼ cup of bourbon. Add this mixture to the yeast sponge and whisk until thoroughly blended. Cover, and let rise for 15 minutes.

3. Oil muffin tins. Use a small ladle to fill the muffin cups to the three-fourths level. The batter will be soft and fluffy. Bang the tin on the counter to settle the dough into the cups. Bake for 10 minutes, then brush the tops with the remaining tablespoon of bourbon. Bake for another 5 minutes or until nicely puffed and a dark golden brown. Cool for 5 minutes in the pan, remove, and glaze, if desired.

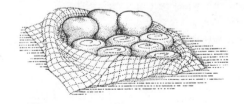

No-Knead Dill Bread

Because of the weight of the cottage cheese, this dough is given a single rise. But like several other breads, the dough has extra yeast and is placed in a cold oven to aid the slow leavening process. Once the dough begins to bake, the perky smell of dill fills the house with its herby aroma. This moist loaf makes superior sandwiches and exceptional toast.

Makes one 8- or 9-inch round bread (1¼ pounds)

> 1 package proofable fast-rising yeast (2 teaspoons)
>   *(see yeast note, page 5)*
> pinch of sugar
> pinch of thyme
> ¼ cup warm water
> 1 cup small-curd cottage cheese
> 1½ tablespoons butter
> 2 tablespoons honey
> 1 teaspoon dried onion soup
> 2 teaspoons dill weed
> ¼ teaspoon baking soda
> 1 teaspoon salt
> 1 egg, beaten
> 2¼ to 2½ cups all-purpose flour

1. Sprinkle the yeast, sugar, and thyme in a large mixing bowl, add the warm water, and stir to dissolve the yeast. Put the bowl aside in a warm spot. Meanwhile, heat the cottage cheese, 1 tablespoon of butter, and the honey in a saucepan over medium heat until the mixture is lukewarm and the but-

ter melts. Remove the pan from the heat and stir in the onion soup, dill weed, baking soda, and salt. Stir to blend all the flavorings and check the temperature; it should not exceed 115 degrees. If it does, stir for a minute or so.

2. Scrape the cottage cheese mixture into the yeast mixture, add the egg, and stir. Add 2 cups of flour and stir with a wooden spoon. Slowly add enough of the remaining flour to produce a soft ball of dough that is not sticky. Gather the dough together with your hand to form a ball. Soak a cloth in hot water, wring it out, and place it over the mixing bowl. Put the bowl in a warm spot for 30 minutes.

3. Meanwhile, generously grease an 8- or 9-inch round pan; a cake pan is fine. Stir down the dough and scrape it into the greased pan, patting to smooth the surface a little. Place the pan in a cold oven, turn on the heat to 350 degrees, and bake for about 35 minutes or until the top is nicely browned and a toothpick plunged into the center comes out clean. The precise timing will depend on how rapidly the oven reaches 350 degrees.

4. Cool the bread for 5 minutes, then turn it out onto a rack. Melt the remaining ½ tablespoon of butter and brush it over the top of the hot bread to give it a shiny crust.

Dill Loaf Variation

Follow directions for the above No-Knead Dill Bread but eliminate the dried onion soup and increase dill weed to 2 tablespoons. Grease a loaf pan, fit a piece of wax or parchment paper in the bottom, and grease it well. Allow the dough to rise a second time in the loaf pan for 15 minutes and bake in a preheated 350-degree oven for about 20 minutes.

Two-Cheese Bread

Both cottage cheese and sharp cheddar are incorporated into this special bread that would make exceptional cold lamb or ham sandwiches.

Makes one loaf (1½ pounds)

> 1 package proofable fast-rising yeast (2 teaspoons)
>   *(see yeast note, page 5)*
> ¼ teaspoon sugar
> pinch of ginger
> ¼ cup warm water
> 1 cup cottage cheese
> 2 tablespoons butter
> 2 tablespoons honey
> ¼ teaspoon baking soda
> 1 teaspoon salt
> about 2½ cups all-purpose flour
> 1 egg, beaten
> 4 ounces sharp cheddar cheese, diced

1. In a large mixing bowl stir the yeast, sugar, and ginger in the warm water. Put aside in a warm spot. In a saucepan heat the cottage cheese, 1 tablespoon of butter, and the honey until lukewarm. Add the baking soda and salt and stir for half a minute. Add ½ cup flour and stir.

2. Scrape the cottage cheese mixture into the yeast, add the egg, and beat well. Add enough of the remaining flour to

make a firm ball of dough; stir with a wooden spoon but do not knead. Sprinkle on the cheddar cheese and fold it into the dough. Soak a cloth in hot water, wring it out, and place over the bowl. Let the dough rise in a warm place for 30 minutes.

3. Cut a strip of wax paper to fit the bottom of a loaf pan. Grease the pan, fit the paper in, and grease the paper. Stir down the dough and scrape it into the pan, patting to smooth the top.

4. Place the loaf pan in the oven, turn on the heat to 350 degrees, and bake for about 45 minutes or until the top is nicely browned and the bread feels firm. Cool the bread for 5 minutes in the pan, turn out, pull off the paper, and place on a rack. To achieve a shiny crust, melt the remaining table-spoon of butter and brush over the top. Cool on a rack.

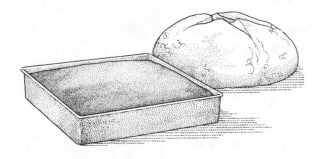

Parsley-Parmesan Bread

The marriage of parsley and Parmesan cheese is a particularly happy one. The cheese is not so strong and assertive that it mutes the soft, herby flavor of the parsley. Speaking of liaisons, match this bread with ham or tongue for a stellar sandwich.

Makes one loaf (1½ pounds)

> 1 package proofable fast-rising yeast (2 teaspoons)
>   *(see yeast note, page 5)*
> ¼ teaspoon sugar
> pinch of nutmeg
> ¼ cup warm water
> 1 cup cottage cheese
> 2 tablespoons butter
> 2 tablespoons honey
> 1 teaspoon fennel seeds
> 1 teaspoon salt ·
> 1 egg, beaten
> about 2½ cups all-purpose flour
> ¾ cup freshly grated Parmesan cheese
> ½ teaspoon ground coriander
> ¼ teaspoon baking soda
> 2 cups parsley leaves

1. In a small bowl stir together the yeast, sugar, and nutmeg; add the warm water and stir to dissolve the yeast granules. Put aside in a warm spot. In a saucepan heat together

the cottage cheese, 1 tablespoon of butter, honey, fennel, and salt. Warm just enough to melt the butter, then scrape the mixture into a large mixing bowl and stir to cool to luke-warm. Add the yeast, then the egg, and stir to mix all the ingredients thoroughly.

2. Add about 2¼ cups of the flour and stir with a wooden spoon; add the remaining ¼ cup flour, a tablespoon at a time, until the dough is fairly stiff. Gather the dough into a ball with your fingers. Soak a towel in hot water and wring it out, drape it over the bowl, and place in a warm spot for 30 minutes.

3. Meanwhile, measure the cheese, coriander, and baking soda into a small cup and mix with your fingers; put aside. Chop the parsley and melt the remaining tablespoon of butter. Also prepare a loaf pan by cutting a piece of parchment or wax paper to fit the bottom, smear oil inside the pan, place the paper in the bottom, and move it around to coat it thoroughly with the oil, then flip the paper over.

4. Stir down the risen dough while sprinkling on the cheese mixture and the parsley. Scrape the dough into the prepared pan; smooth the top and tap the pan sharply on the counter to settle the dough well into the bottom. If the batter does not spread easily, dip a rubber spatula in cold water and run it over the top.

5. Place the pan in a cold oven, turn on the heat to 350 degrees, and bake for about 45 minutes or until the top is nicely browned and a toothpick plunged into the center comes out clean. Remove the pan from the oven, allow to cool for 5 minutes, then turn out the loaf, pull off the paper, and place the loaf on a rack. Brush the top with the melted butter.

Bacon-Cheese Pinwheel

This wonderful loaf offers a contrast in textures. Against the soft bread and smooth cheese, one bites into crunchy bits of crisp bacon. Double the recipe and use the extra loaf as a snack—a ready-made bacon-and-cheese sandwich. Toasted, it's another treat.

Makes one loaf (1¼ pounds)

> 1 teaspoon proofable fast-rising yeast
> *(see yeast note, page 5)*
> 1 tablespoon sugar, plus ¼ teaspoon
> pinch of ginger
> 1 cup warm water
> about 2½ cups bread flour
> ½ teaspoon salt
> ¼ teaspoon vinegar
> ¼ pound sliced bacon
> 2 ounces sharp cheddar cheese
> 1 egg, beaten

1. Follow the directions for Sandwich Bread I (Food Processor) (page 114). While the dough is rising, slowly fry the bacon until crisp and drain on paper towels; when cool, crumble into a small bowl. Grate the cheese into the bowl and mix the bacon and cheese together. Grease a loaf pan.

2. Punch down the risen dough and place it on a lightly floured work surface. Either pat with your hands, or gently

roll the dough into a rectangle about 10 × 14 inches. Brush the dough very well with the beaten egg, then sprinkle the bacon and cheese over the dough, leaving clear about ½ inch at the edges. Lift one of the shorter edges and roll the dough tightly; pinch the seam closed. Transfer the roll to the loaf pan, squeezing a little to make it fit if it is too long. Cover with plastic wrap and put in a warm place to rise for 30 minutes.

Preheat oven to 425 degrees.

3. Just before putting the pan in the oven, brush the top with the beaten egg. Bake for 10 minutes, then reduce the heat to 350 degrees, and bake about 20 minutes or more. Remove from the pan and rap on the bottom; if it sounds hollow the loaf is baked. Cool on a rack.

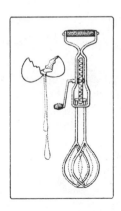

Giant Popovers

Strange as it may seem, the least satisfactory way to bake popovers is in the traditional cast-iron mold. A lot of steam is
necessary to encourage the rolls to puff enthusiastically. The
classic mold is compact, and because of the concentration of
steam the popovers in the center are prevented from rising
evenly and developing crisp exteriors. A very unattractive
modern cast-iron mold solves this problem by spreading the
cups out in spider fashion. I find large pottery cups the best
baking vehicle, and they can be used for other purposes. If
you do not have the large cups, use twice as many custard
cups and reduce baking time by about 15 minutes. Metal
pans should be buttered and preheated.

Makes eight giant or sixteen regular popovers

      8 6-ounce pottery baking cups
      6 eggs, room temperature
      2 cups milk, room temperature
      6 tablespoons butter, melted
      2 cups sifted all-purpose flour
      1 teaspoon salt

Preheat oven to 375 degrees.

1. Liberally butter the cups and arrange them on a sturdy
baking sheet with at least 2 inches of space between them.
Break the eggs into a mixing bowl and beat them lightly with
an electric or hand beater. Continue beating while adding the

milk and the melted butter. Beat in the flour and salt. The batter should be the consistency of whipping cream.

2. Pour the batter into a pitcher and fill each of the buttered cups to the two-thirds level and bake for 1 hour. *Do not* open the oven door at any time while the popovers are baking. Remove the popovers from the oven and quickly cut a slit on the side of each one. Return the popovers to the oven, turn off the heat, and let them crisp for 5 minutes. The tops will be very firm, crisp, and a deep brown. Popovers that are not baked enough will collapse.

3. To remove the popovers from the cups, turn them upside down and shake into your hand. If they will not come out even with a little tug on the puffed top, slide the tip of a grapefruit knife across the bottom and lift them out. Serve at once while the popovers are piping hot.

Cheese Popovers

Cheddar cheese works beautifully in this recipe, but my preference is for Parmesan. I find that its flavor does not overwhelm the buttery quality of the popovers. Try it both ways.

Makes eight giant or sixteen regular popovers

6 eggs, room temperature
2 cups milk, room temperature
6 tablespoons butter, melted
2 cups sifted all-purpose flour
1 teaspoon salt
½ cup grated Parmesan or cheddar cheese
½ teaspoon paprika

Preheat oven to 375 degrees.

Follow the directions for Giant Popovers (page 142). Add the cheese and paprika to the completed batter and stir briefly.

Maple-Cinnamon Popovers

Because of the dark flavorings added to this batter, once baked, the hot popover has a dark crust and a dusky interior. The enticing aroma that pours forth from the oven will sharply whet appetites.

Makes eight giant or sixteen regular popovers

> 6 eggs, room temperature
> ¼ cup pure maple syrup
> 1 teaspoon cinnamon
> 1 teaspoon vanilla
> 2 cups milk, room temperature
> 6 tablespoons butter, melted
> 2 cups sifted all-purpose flour
> 1 teaspoon salt

Preheat oven to 375 degrees.

Follow directions for Giant Popovers (page 142) and add ingredients to the bowl in the order listed above.

Boston Brown Bread

Traditional Boston Brown Bread is cooked by steam. The usual method requires at least three hours of steaming, but anyone with a pressure cooker can turn out the dusky cylinders in less than one and a half hours, from beginning to end. A one-pound coffee can is the most often used container for the batter; however, it will not fit most four-quart pressure cookers. It is fine in six-quart cookers. I found that two fourteen-ounce soup, or similar, cans will hold the same amount of batter.

Makes one 2-pound loaf or two 1-pound loaves

½ cup raisins
½ cup cornmeal, yellow or white
½ cup rye flour
½ cup whole wheat flour
1 teaspoon baking soda
½ teaspoon salt
1 cup buttermilk
⅓ cup unsulfured molasses

1. Cover the raisins with hot water, let stand for 15 minutes, and drain well. Meanwhile, select either a 1-pound coffee can or two 14-ounce soup cans depending on the depth of your pressure cooker. Cut parchment paper rounds to fit the bottom. Oil the cans very well, fit the paper in, flip the paper, and press it down.

2. Combine the cornmeal and the rye and whole wheat flours in a mixing bowl and stir in the baking soda and salt. In another bowl beat the buttermilk and molasses and add to the dry ingredients, beating vigorously with a wooden spoon. Add raisins and beat again; fill cans to three-quarters level. Butter squares of heavy-duty foil and place over cans, greased side down, press foil against the cans firmly, and close tightly with string; cut off excess string. Fold the foil back so it does not reach the middle of the can.

3. Place the cans on a rack in the pressure cooker and add enough water to come halfway up the sides of the can—no more. Put on the cooker cover, lock into position, and put on high heat. When a jet of steam comes through the vent, reduce the heat to low and cook—without pressure—for 20 minutes. Put on the pressure gauge and turn up the heat. When the gauge reaches 15 pounds of pressure, reduce the heat and steam the bread for 50 minutes.

4. Remove the cans from the cooker, let stand for 10 minutes to allow the steam to subside, then turn out and peel off the parchment paper. Slice across in rounds and serve warm with lots of butter.

Olive Mosaic Bread

The term *mosaic* is applied to this loaf because of the attractive pattern produced by the black olives, pimientoes, and nuts. Each slice is studded with the black, red, and tan colors of the three garnishes. The emphatic flavor of the bread could even qualify it as a cocktail tidbit.

Makes one loaf (1½ pounds)

½ cup chopped black olives
½ cup chopped pimientoes
3 tablespoons butter, softened
¼ cup sugar
2 eggs
2 cups all-purpose flour
1 tablespoon baking powder
¼ teaspoon baking soda
½ teaspoon salt
½ teaspoon dry mustard
¾ cup milk
½ cup chopped walnuts

Preheat oven to 350 degrees.

1. Put the olives in a small strainer and rinse under cold water. Press out as much water as possible and put aside to drain. Put the pimientoes in a small strainer, press out as much of the oil as possible, and put aside. Grease a loaf pan, fit a piece of wax or parchment paper in the bottom, and grease it as well.

2. Thoroughly cream the butter and sugar together. Add the eggs, one at a time, and beat well between each addition. Put the flour, baking powder, baking soda, salt, and dry mustard into a sifter and sift the dry ingredients into the bowl alternating with the milk, about one-third at a time. Blend well after each addition. Finally, stir in the olives, pimientoes, and nuts and scrape the batter into the prepared loaf pan.

3. Bake for about 50 minutes or until nicely puffed and brown and a toothpick plunged into the center comes out clean. Cool in the pan for 10 minutes, then turn out onto a rack. Cool completely before slicing.

Portuguese Corn Bread (Broa)

Like most corn breads, *broa* usually accompanies dishes with lots of sauce. Although corn breads are no novelty to Americans, this Portuguese classic is quite different in that it is leavened with yeast, which guarantees smooth, noncrumbly slices.

Makes one 9-inch round loaf (1¼ pounds)

> 1 package proofable fast-rising yeast (2 teaspoons)
>   *(see yeast note, page 5)*
> 2 tablespoons sugar, plus ¼ teaspoon
> pinch of nutmeg
> ¼ cup warm water
> 1 cup cold water
> 1½ cups cornmeal
> 1 teaspoon salt
> 2 tablespoons olive oil
> about 2 cups all-purpose flour

1. Stir the yeast, ¼ teaspoon sugar, and the nutmeg together in a small bowl, pour in the warm water, stir, and put aside in a warm spot. Meanwhile, bring the cold water to a full boil while measuring into a mixing bowl 1 cup of cornmeal, salt, and the remaining 2 tablespoons sugar. Stir in the boiling water and beat until the mixture is thick and smooth. Add the olive oil and blend it in.

2. Stir in 1 cup of the flour and beat for a few seconds. Feel the mixture and make certain it isn't too hot—above 115 degrees—before adding the foamy yeast mixture. After the yeast has been incorporated, blend in the final half-cup of cornmeal. Beat the batter for a minute, oil your hands, and pat it into a ball. Cover the bowl with a damp cloth and place in a warm spot for 30 minutes.

3. Grease a 9-inch pie dish and put aside. Put the remaining cup of flour in a dish and sprinkle about a quarter of it onto a pastry board. Scrape the dough onto the board and knead it for 5 minutes, incorporating as much of the flour as necessary to produce a firm dough that remains slightly sticky. Usually the full 2 cups are needed, but this will depend on the protein quality of the brand of flour. Oil your hands again and pat the dough into a round, flat loaf and place it in the greased pie dish. Brush some olive oil over the surface, cover, and let rise another 15 minutes.

Preheat oven to 350 degrees.

4. Bake for about 30 minutes or until the top is lightly colored and the bread begins to pull away from the dish. Cool for 5 minutes, then turn out onto a rack to cool or serve warm.

Light Pumpkin Bread

Light does not refer to the color of this round loaf but to its texture. Leavened with beaten egg whites, the finished bread has an almost spongy quality.

Makes one deep 6-inch round loaf (1¾ pounds)

> 1 cup milk
> 1 tablespoon butter, diced
> ¼ cup sugar
> ½ teaspoon salt
> 1 cup pumpkin purée
> 3 eggs, room temperature
> ½ teaspoon vanilla
> ¼ teaspoon mace
> 1 cup all-purpose flour
> 1 cup cornmeal
> large pinch of cream of tartar

Preheat oven to 400 degrees.

1. In a small pot heat together the milk, butter, sugar, and salt. Once the butter has melted, remove the pot from the heat, stir for a few seconds, and put aside. Select a 6-cup soufflé or similar dish and cut a round of parchment or wax paper to fit the bottom. Liberally butter the dish, fit the paper in the bottom, and butter it.

2. Put the pumpkin in a mixing bowl. Separate the eggs, dropping the yolks onto the pumpkin and the whites into an-

other clean bowl. Add the vanilla and mace to the pumpkin and whisk together. While continuing to whisk, pour in the warm milk mixture. Add the flour and cornmeal and beat well to blend all the ingredients thoroughly. The batter will be fairly stiff.

3. Beat the egg whites for a few seconds until they begin to froth, add the cream of tartar, and beat them until they are thick and firm but not dry. Scoop about one-third of the whites over the batter and thoroughly blend the whites into the batter to lighten it. Give a few extra strokes to the beaten whites, scrape them over the batter, and gently fold them in with a rubber spatula; it is far better to leave a few visible bubbles of white than to break them down.

4. Scrape the batter into the prepared mold, smooth the surface, and place in the hot oven. Immediately turn down the temperature to 375 degrees and bake for about 1 hour or until the bread is well puffed and shows a few cracks; a sharp knife plunged into the center should come out clean. Cool for 5 minutes, then turn out of the dish and pull off the paper. Cool on a rack. Light Pumpkin Bread is best eaten warm or at room temperature.

Tyrolean Flatbread

A number of flatbread recipes are included on these pages for several reasons. They are not mysterious creations that require any special touch or feel; they have great keeping ability, and they can be made easily and quickly. Furthermore, flatbreads deliver a range of interesting textures and flavors.

Makes eight 6-inch flatbreads

> 1 package proofable fast-rising yeast (2 teaspoons)
>   *(see yeast note, page 5)*
> ½ teaspoon sugar
> large pinch of ginger
> ½ cup warm water
> ⅔ cup milk
> ⅔ cup cold water
> ¼ teaspoon anise seeds
> 1 tablespoon caraway seeds
> 2 cups rye flour
> about 1½ cups all-purpose flour
> 2 teaspoons salt

1. Put the yeast, sugar, ginger, and warm water in a large mixing bowl; stir and put aside in a warm spot for 5 minutes. Meanwhile, grease another mixing bowl.

2. Scald the milk, add the cold water, and, before combining it with the yeast, check that the temperature is below 115 degrees. Flavor the mixture with the anise and caraway seeds,

then stir in the rye flour and 1 cup all-purpose flour. Liberally flour a pastry board, pull the dough onto it, and knead for 5 minutes while adding just enough of the remaining half-cup of flour to produce a stiff dough that does not stick to the board or your hands. Spread the dough out, sprinkle with the salt, and knead an additional minute. Drop the dough into the greased bowl, turn to coat all surfaces, cover with a damp cloth, and put aside to rise for 40 minutes.

Preheat oven to 400 degrees.

3. Grease two sturdy baking sheets. Punch the dough down and separate into eight pieces. Place a piece of dough on a square of wax paper and pound it with the side of your fist into a circle about 6 inches round. Flip the sheet of wax paper onto the baking sheet and pull it away from the flatbread. Smooth the surface and score into quarters with the tip of a sharp knife dipped in flour. When all the rounds have been made, cover the baking sheets with plastic wrap and let rise for 20 minutes in a warm spot.

4. Bake the flatbreads for 15 minutes or until they feel firm. Slide them onto racks to cool.

Norwegian Potato Flatbread (Lefse)

Unlike most other thin flatbreads, which fry into crisp rounds, *lefse* is soft. In the traditional form it is folded into quarters. A grooved *lefse* rolling pin is also traditional, but a smooth pin will do just as well. The final result will not be as decorative, but the flavor is deliciously identical.

Makes eight 10-inch rounds

> 2 pounds russet potatoes
> 2 tablespoons butter, cut into pieces
> ¼ cup light cream
> 1 teaspoon salt
> about 1 cup all-purpose flour

1. Scrub the potatoes and boil in water until they can be easily pierced with a knife, about 20 minutes. Peel the potatoes as soon as you can handle them and drop them into a large mixing bowl that contains the butter, cream, and salt. Mash the potatoes until they are smooth.

2. Stir in enough flour to make a smooth dough. Cover and let rest for 15 minutes. Divide the dough into eight balls and roll each one on a lightly floured board into a very thin round about 10 inches across. Keep the remaining dough covered. Depending on how quickly you roll the dough, begin frying when two or three disks are ready and continue to roll and fry.

3. Heat a heavy ungreased cast-iron skillet or griddle until hot, slip in one round, and fry for about 1 minute or until the bottom is liberally flecked with brown. Turn with a long, thin spatula and fry the other side. If the *lefse* is turned over several times during the frying, it will become crisp; the supple texture is more traditional.

4. As each *lefse* is removed from the pan, fold it into quarters and stack in a covered napkin-lined dish. Additional butter can be served to smear on the inside.

Indian Whole Wheat Griddle Flatbread (Chappati)

A curry dinner is not traditional without *chappati*—hot paper-thin rounds of whole wheat goodness. Indian recipes specify whole wheat flour only, but some adaptations include a little all-purpose flour to facilitate rolling the dough. That is the route followed here. Another change from the classic is to include some fat, which allows the fried *chappati* to wait for a longer period of time before serving.

Makes about eight 5-inch flatbreads

> 2 cups whole wheat flour
> ½ cup all-purpose flour
> 1 teaspoon salt
> 4 tablespoons butter, melted
> about ¾ cup warm water

1. Combine the flours and salt in a mixing bowl and sprinkle over them the melted butter and half a cup of water. Stir with a fork, then knead, adding just enough additional water, a tablespoon at a time, to make a firm but supple dough. Knead for 10 minutes, cover with a damp cloth, and let the dough rest for 30 minutes. (At this point the dough can wait for several hours, even overnight. For periods longer than 1 hour, refrigerate the dough.)

2. Separate the dough into eight small rounds and flatten each round with your hands, then on a lightly floured board roll the dough into paper-thin rounds about 8 inches in diameter. During the rolling, turn the rounds over so that both sides are floured. Stack the rounds until you are ready to fry them.

3. Heat a heavy cast-iron griddle or skillet until medium hot and fry the *chappati* one at a time, about 2 minutes per side, turning the flatbreads over when the bottom is flecked with brown.

4. Line a deep dish with napkins and stack the fried *chappati* in it; keep the top covered to retain as much heat as possible.

Oatmeal-Date Loaf

When working with this batter you might think it a trifle thin. It should be. Both the oatmeal and the wheat germ absorb liquid during baking, and the end result is perfect.

Makes one loaf (1½ pounds)

1 egg
⅓ cup honey
⅓ cup sugar
¼ cup butter, melted
¾ cup regular rolled oats
1½ cups all-purpose flour
1 teaspoon baking powder
½ teaspoon baking soda
½ teaspoon salt
1 cup buttermilk
⅓ cup wheat germ
⅓ cup chopped dates or raisins

Preheat oven to 350 degrees.

1. Oil a loaf pan, fit a piece of wax or parchment paper on the bottom, move the paper around a little, and flip it over. In a large mixing bowl whisk together the egg, honey, and sugar until very well blended. Pour in the butter and whisk a few seconds more, then stir in the rolled oats. Put the flour, baking powder, baking soda, and salt in a sifter and sift into the bowl alternately with the buttermilk. Finally, stir in the wheat germ and dates or raisins.

2. Pour the batter into the prepared pan and bake for about 55 minutes or until a toothpick plunged into the center comes out clean. Cool for 10 minutes in the pan, then remove to a rack.

Orange-Raisin Bread

Orange is a very accommodating fruit for bread makers. It needs no supporting cast to deliver knockout flavor, but it does not overwhelm garnishes such as sweet butter, jam, honey, or even cottage cheese. Though either dark or white raisins can be used, the pale variety harmonizes better with the golden loaf.

Makes one loaf (1¾ pounds)

> 1 teaspoon proofable fast-rising yeast
> *(see yeast note, page 5)*
> ¼ cup sugar, plus ¼ teaspoon
> large pinch of nutmeg
> ¼ cup warm water
> ½ cup raisins, preferably white
> 2 tablespoons orange liqueur
> ¾ cup orange juice
> 1 cup quick-cooking oatmeal
> 2 tablespoons oil
> ¼ cup dried skim milk
> 1 teaspoon grated orange rind
> 3 cups all-purpose flour
> 2 eggs, beaten
> ½ teaspoon salt

1. In a small bowl mix the yeast, ¼ teaspoon sugar, nutmeg, and warm water; put aside in a warm spot. Put the raisins in a small cup, pour in the liqueur, mix, and set aside.

Grease a loaf pan, fit a piece of parchment or wax paper in the bottom, and grease it.

2. Heat the orange juice to lukewarm while measuring into a large mixing bowl the oatmeal, ¼ cup sugar, oil, dried milk, orange rind, and ½ cup flour. Pour the orange juice into the bowl and beat well. Add the foamy yeast and beat for 1 minute. Stir in the eggs, the remaining 2½ cups flour, and the salt and beat vigorously with a wooden spoon for 5 minutes. Add the raisins and liqueur and beat for 1 more minute.

3. Scrape the batter into the prepared loaf pan; it will be stiff and uncooperative and require real scraping. Smooth the top with a spatula moistened with warm water, then brush with oil. Cover with a cloth soaked in hot water and wrung out and place in a warm spot to rise for 30 minutes.

Preheat oven to 375 degrees.

4. Bake the loaf for about 35 minutes or until the top is nicely browned and a small, sharp knife plunged into the side comes out clean. Cool in the pan for 5 minutes, then turn out onto a rack.

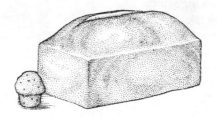

Banana-Nut Bread

An all-time favorite, Banana Bread—with or without nuts—is a snap to make. The flavor is best if very ripe bananas are used.

Makes one loaf (1¾ pounds)

> ½ cup butter, softened
> ¾ cup sugar
> 2 eggs
> 1½ cups mashed bananas (about 2 medium)
> 2 cups all-purpose flour
> ½ teaspoon baking soda
> ½ teaspoon salt
> ½ cup chopped nuts—walnuts, pecans, or filberts; or ¼
>   cup wheat germ

Preheat oven to 350 degrees.

1. Cream the butter well and slowly add the sugar. The more thoroughly you cream this mixture the lighter the bread will be. Add the eggs, one at a time, and beat well between each addition. Stir in the mashed bananas.

2. Put the flour, baking soda, and salt into a sifter and sift about one-third of the dry ingredients into a large mixing bowl. Stir in about one-third of the creamed mixture and repeat twice more. After the final addition, sprinkle in the nuts or wheat germ and stir well to blend but do not beat.

3. Grease a loaf pan, fit a piece of wax or parchment paper on the bottom, and grease it as well. Scrape the batter into the pan and place in the oven for about 1 hour or until the loaf is puffed and nicely browned and a toothpick plunged into the center comes out clean. Cool in the pan for 10 minutes, then turn out onto a rack. Cool completely before slicing.

Orange-Nut Loaf

Just a hint of sweetness is added to this loaf, which means it can be served at mealtime as well as a snack anytime.

Makes one loaf (1¼ pounds)

> 2 oranges
> 2 cups all-purpose flour
> ¼ cup sugar
> 1½ teaspoons baking powder
> ½ teaspoon baking soda
> 1 teaspoon salt
> ½ teaspoon ground coriander
> ¼ teaspoon ginger
> 4 tablespoons cold butter, diced
> 1 egg
> ½ cup orange juice
> ½ cup milk
> ½ cup walnuts, coarsely chopped

Preheat oven to 350 degrees.

1. Cut a piece of parchment or wax paper to fit the bottom of an overproof glass loaf dish. Oil the dish, put in the paper, move it around a little, and flip it over. Grate the rind of the oranges taking care not to include any of the bitter white pith; there should be about 1 tablespoon. Sift into a mixing bowl the flour, sugar, baking powder, baking soda, and salt. Add the grated orange rind, coriander, and ginger and stir to

distribute the flavorings. Add the butter and work with a pastry blender or two knives to reduce the butter to small bits; the mixture should look like coarse meal.

2. In a small bowl beat together the egg, orange juice, and milk and stir into the dry ingredients. Scatter the nuts over the batter and mix in briefly. Scrape the batter into the prepared loaf dish and bake for about 45 minutes or until the top is puffed and golden brown and a toothpick plunged into the center emerges dry. Cool in the dish for 15 minutes, then turn out onto a rack to cool completely.

PART FOUR

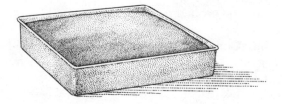

Great Fast Breads in Less Than Two Hours

Great Fast Breads
in Less Than Two Hours

Ryebread Rolls

Thanks to a combination of flours, these rolls are much more versatile than if made with rye flour alone. They make an admirable dinner roll, and the milder flavor readily accommodates almost any sandwich filling.

Makes eighteen 2½-inch rolls

> 1 package proofable fast-rising yeast (2 teaspoons)
>   *(see yeast note, page 5)*
> 3 tablespoons sugar
> ⅛ teaspoon nutmeg
> ¼ cup warm water
> about 3¼ cups all-purpose flour
> 2 cups rye flour
> 1 tablespoon caraway seeds
> 2 teaspoons salt
> 1 cup milk
> ¾ cup water
> 1 tablespoon butter

1. In a small bowl stir together the yeast, ½ teaspoon sugar, and nutmeg with the warm water and put aside in a warm spot. Meanwhile, in a large bowl measure 2¼ cups of the all-purpose flour, all the rye flour, caraway seeds, salt, and the remaining sugar. Oil another bowl and set aside.

2. In a small pot heat the milk, water, and butter to lukewarm or just until the butter melts. Pour the milk over the

dry ingredients; the batter should feel lukewarm. Scrape in the yeast and thoroughly blend it into the dough. Mix in enough of the remaining cup of all-purpose flour to make a soft dough. Knead the dough on a floured board for 5 minutes, gather into a ball, and throw it against the board ten or fifteen times. Drop the dough into the greased bowl, turn it over to coat with the oil, cover with a hot, damp cloth, and put aside in a warm spot for 30 minutes.

Preheat oven to 375 degrees.

3. Punch down the dough, turn out onto a floured board, and knead just ten times. Grease a baking sheet. Pull off about ⅓ cup of dough and roll between the palms of your hands to form a ball; place on the baking sheet. Continue with the remaining dough, cover again with plastic wrap, and put aside in a warm spot for 15 minutes.

4. Bake the rolls for about 30 minutes or until the crust is a dark tan and feels firm. Cool on a rack.

English Muffins

The interior of these English Muffins is akin to traditional homemade rolls in England, where the small pan-fried breads were known by a variety of names before they became "muffins." Commercial muffins have a puffier, craggier interior that we have become accustomed to. In the process we've lost the inviting, yeasty flavor of the original. Have it again.

Makes twelve 3-inch muffins

> 1 package proofable fast-rising yeast (2 teaspoons)
>   *(see yeast note, page 5)*
> 1 tablespoon sugar
> large pinch of ginger
> ¼ cup warm water
> 1 cup milk
> 3 tablespoons butter, cut into pieces
> 1 teaspoon salt
> about 4 cups all-purpose flour
> Optional: about ¼ cup yellow cornmeal

1. Put the yeast, ½ teaspoon sugar, and ginger in a small bowl. Add the warm water, stir, and put aside in a warm spot. In the meantime, scald the milk, but do not bring it to a full boil. Put the butter, remaining 2½ teaspoons of sugar, and the salt into a large mixing bowl, pour the hot milk into the bowl, and stir to melt the butter.

2. Add 2 cups of flour to the bowl and stir until the batter is lukewarm, then stir in the foamy yeast and beat vigorously with a wooden spoon for 2 minutes. Add another cup of flour and beat until it is well blended, then turn the dough onto a well-floured board. Knead the dough until it is soft but not sticky, adding as much of the remaining cup of flour as necessary. Grease a bowl, drop the dough into it, and put aside in a warm spot for 30 minutes.

3. Punch down the dough and break off half of it. Roll the dough on a lightly floured board to ½-inch thickness. Cut the dough into 2½-inch rounds. If coating the muffins, pour the cornmeal into a small dish, dip both sides of the muffins in the cornmeal, and pat lightly to press the grain into the muffin. Add the leftover trimmings to the other half of the dough, roll it out, and continue to make more muffins. Gather and rework the trimmings until all the dough is used. Place the muffins on a baking sheet, cover with plastic wrap, and let rise in a warm spot for 15 minutes.

4. Preheat a griddle or a heavy cast-iron skillet until warm but not super-hot. Spread about ½ tablespoon oil over the griddle and place muffin rounds around the outer edge only if using a gas range. On an electric range the muffins can be placed in the center as well. The idea is to cook the muffins at a steady, medium-hot temperature, and the center of a gas burner can be a hot spot. Do not crowd the muffins but allow room for expansion. Once the muffins are in the pan, turn the heat down to low. Cook the muffins for about 10 minutes, turning them 180 degrees after about 5 minutes to brown the bottom evenly. Turn and repeat with the other side. The muffins will rise somewhat and take on a floury look. Remove the cooked muffins, wipe off the griddle or skillet to remove excess cornmeal, reheat, oil the griddle, and continue with another batch. Cool the muffins on a rack.

5. English Muffins should be pulled apart or split with a fork, then toasted.

Note: These muffins can also be baked in a 400-degree oven for about 15 minutes, turning them over when half-baked. The neat, round shape of the muffins will be sacrificed though, and they will become puffy and round.

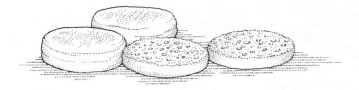

Steamed Maple-Oatmeal Bread

The bread most often steamed is Boston Brown Bread (page 146) but there are other possibilities for the moist cooking method. This particular bread has a milder flavor, which makes it more adaptable as a mealtime accompaniment. See the note about bread sizes in the introduction to the Boston Brown Bread recipe.

Makes one 2-pound loaf or two 1-pound loaves

1 cup regular oatmeal
1½ cups buttermilk
½ cup pure maple syrup
1 cup whole wheat flour
1 cup yellow cornmeal
½ teaspoon baking soda
½ teaspoon salt
½ cup raisins
1 tablespoon all-purpose flour

1. Put the oatmeal, buttermilk, and maple syrup in a mixing bowl, stir, and put aside for about 30 minutes. Meanwhile, oil the baking cans, fit a piece of parchment paper in the bottom, and oil it.

2. Sift into the oatmeal base the whole wheat flour, cornmeal, baking soda, and salt. Stir with a wooden spoon until the dry and liquid ingredients are thoroughly blended. Toss

the raisins with the all-purpose flour, add to the batter, and stir briefly.

3. Spoon the batter into the prepared cans. Cut heavy-duty aluminum foil sheets to fit the tops of the cans with plenty of overlap. Grease the foil and place over the cans, greased side down. Crimp the foil against the cans, then tie very tightly with string. Cut off excess string and fold back the foil so that it is above the halfway line but with a good overhang.

4. Steam according to the directions for Boston Brown Bread (page 146) allowing 15 minutes pre-pressure cooking and 50 minutes with 15 pounds pressure. Cool in cans for 10 minutes, cut around the bread with a flexible knife, and gently shake out. Cool on a rack.

Ham-and-Cheese Stollen

The typical *stollen* is a sweet bread, and the recipe on page 202 is a quick and easy version of it. I decided to use the same streamlined preparation to produce a savory loaf. This novel roll is delicious at room temperature but is even better sliced and warmed in the oven.

Makes one *stollen* (¾ pounds)

> ¼ pound sharp cheddar cheese
> 1 thick slice ham, about ¼ pound
> 2¼ cups all-purpose flour
> 1½ tablespoons baking powder
> ½ teaspoon salt
> 2 tablespoons lard, softened
> 4 tablespoons butter, softened
> 1 tablespoon sugar
> ¼ teaspoon cardamom
> ¼ teaspoon anise seeds
> 1 egg
> 1 cup cottage cheese, sieved
> 1 tablespoon butter, melted

Preheat oven to 350 degrees.

1. Cut the cheese and ham into tiny dice, about ⅛-inch square. Sift the flour, baking powder, and salt onto a pastry board. Make a well in the center and in it put the lard, butter, sugar, cardamom, and anise seeds. Knead these ingredients

together, then add the egg and cottage cheese and continue to blend together the flavorings and fats. Once they are fairly well amalgamated, begin working in the flour, pulling a little at a time into the center. Before the dough is kneaded into a ball, add the cheese and ham and continue kneading for a minute more. Alternatively, cream the lard, butter, and sugar together in a bowl; add the cardamom, anise, egg, and cottage cheese and whisk all together very well. Scrape this creamed mixture into the well and, little by little, work the flour into the soft ingredients.

2. Roll the dough into a rectangle approximately 16 × 12 inches and 1 inch thick. The dough is now folded into thirds by lifting one of the narrow ends and folding it over two-thirds of the rectangle. Lift the remaining one-third of dough and fold it onto the package. Press lightly. If you are dubious about the instructions, try folding a sheet of paper first.

3. Place the *stollen* on a lightly greased baking sheet and bake for 1 to 1½ hours or until a skewer plunged into the center comes out dry. Transfer to a rack and brush with the melted butter. Cool before cutting.

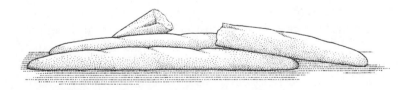

Long French Loaves

I deliberately am not calling this bread a French *baguette* (stick) because it isn't. It also does not take eight hours to produce and pages and pages of instruction. The result after a mere two hours is two delicious loaves with a crackly crust but a closer grain than the original. This bread does not shatter under a knife but slices beautifully. It is advisable to remove rings and watches before beginning.

Makes two 16-inch loaves (½ pound each)

> 1 teaspoon proofable fast-rising yeast
> *(see yeast note, page 5)*
> ½ teaspoon sugar
> pinch of ginger
> 1¼ cups warm water
> about 3 cups bread flour
> ½ teaspoon salt
> Optional: oil or ice water for glazing

1. In a large mixing bowl stir the yeast, sugar, and ginger together, add ¼ cup warm water, stir, and put aside for 5 minutes. Pour in the remaining cup of warm water, 2½ cups flour, and the salt and beat with a wooden spoon until a sticky mass results.

2. Flour a working surface and have about ½ cup flour in a dish nearby. Scrape the dough onto the board and begin to knead while adding flour, a little at a time. Use the flour to dust the board and sprinkle over the dough. Work the dough vigorously. At the beginning, when the dough is very sticky, it is best to use a metal or plastic scraper to lift the dough and slap it down against the counter. Keep pulling and stretching the dough as you work it. Knead for 10 minutes, no less. When an additional ½ cup of flour has been incor-

porated into the dough, it should pull together into a smooth ball. Under your hands the clinging, sticky mass is transformed into a smooth and cohesive dough.

3. Dust the board with flour again, gather the dough into a ball, and *throw* it down hard against the board. Do not be gentle with the dough. Pretend it is someone or something you don't like and take vengeance. Repeat the throwing fifty or sixty times. Oil a mixing bowl, drop the dough into it, flip over several times to coat it well, cover with a cloth soaked in hot water and wrung out, and put in a warm place to rise for 30 minutes.

Preheat oven to 450 degrees.

4. If you have long, fluted loaf pans, grease them with oil or butter, reaching all the way to the top; if you do not have the pans, grease a sturdy baking sheet. Turn the dough onto a clean board with no flour on it and knead just ten times. Gather the dough into a ball and cut in half. Roll the dough against the board to make a rope about 15 inches long and 2 inches in diameter. Use no flour at this stage. Place the rope into the pan or on the sheet. Repeat with the remaining dough. Cover with plastic wrap and place in a warm spot for about 20 minutes.

6. Slash each loaf in four or five places with a very sharp knife or a razor. Do not make deep slashes but at a shallow 45-degree angle. Brush the surface of the loaves with ice water or oil. Ice water will help create steam in the oven and give the loaves a crisp but dull crust. I prefer to brush with oil for a golden, shiny crust. Bake for 15 minutes, reduce the temperature to 350 degrees, turn the pan around, and continue baking for another 20 to 30 minutes or until the bottom of the loaf sounds hollow when rapped. Remove from the pans at once and cool on a rack. If the loaves seem to be getting too dark during the baking, cover loosely with aluminum foil.

Pumpernickel Bread
(Food Processor)

Homemade Pumpernickel Bread has a depth of flavor that
packaged loaves just can't touch. This version is particularly
flavorsome and fine-textured. To speed up the baking time I
tried various methods—hand kneading with both single and
double rises, as well as using the food processor, again with
single and double rises. The food processor method with
two rises produced the best results. But if you don't have the
machine, please don't give up homemade Pumpernickel; just
count on kneading for a good fifteen minutes. Also, if your
machine is an older, smaller model, make half the recipe.

Makes two 8-inch rounds (1¼ pounds each)

> 1 medium potato
> ½ cup cornmeal
> 1½ cups cold water
> 1 package proofable fast-rising yeast (2 teaspoons)
>   (see yeast note, page 5)
> 1 tablespoon sugar, plus ¼ teaspoon
> pinch of ginger
> ¼ cup warm water
> 1 tablespoon butter
> ½ cup unsulfured molasses
> 1 tablespoon salt
> 1 tablespoon caraway seeds
> ¼ cup cocoa
> 2 to 2¼ cups bread flour
> 2 cups rye flour

1. Peel the potato, cut into half-inch pieces, and boil for
about 10 minutes or until soft. Drain and mash the potatoes.

Meanwhile, pour the cornmeal into a saucepan, stir in the cold water to make a smooth mixture, and place on a medium fire to cook slowly; the mush should be thick in about 3 minutes. Meanwhile, stir together the yeast, ¼ teaspoon sugar, and the ginger; add the warm water, stir, and put aside in a warm place.

2. Once the cornmeal mixture is thick, remove from the heat and add the butter, molasses, salt, caraway seeds, cocoa, and the remaining tablespoon of sugar. Stir until the butter is melted, then scrape the dark mixture into the food processor bowl. Add the mashed potatoes and process until the mass is smooth.

3. Add 1 cup of bread flour and process for a few seconds, scrape in the foamy yeast and process for a few seconds more. Add another cup of the bread flour and all the rye flour and process until the dough is thick and shaggy and almost pulls together in a ball. This should take between half a minute and a minute. If the dough seems too soft, sprinkle in an extra ¼ cup of bread flour and process again.

4. Oil a mixing bowl and your hands. Pull the dough out of the processor and onto a floured board, form it into a round ball, drop into the oiled bowl, and flip it over; cover and put in a warm place to rise for 30 minutes.

Preheat oven to 375 degrees.

5. Punch down the dough and form into two 8-inch rounds. Grease a large baking sheet and sprinkle with cornmeal. Place the loaves on the baking sheet with plenty of space between them. Cover with plastic wrap and let rise another 20 minutes in a warm spot.

6. Bake the bread for about 45 minutes or until the loaves sound hollow when rapped on the bottom. Remove to a rack to cool.

Kasha-Raisin Bread

Kasha (toasted buckwheat groats) is a dusky grain that Russian cooks have long admired. It often appears on the breakfast table as hot cereal and is used in all sorts of ways to capitalize on its slightly nutty flavor. Its soft texture blends beautifully into the interior of this admirable loaf.

Makes one loaf (1 pound)

> ½ cup milk
> 3 tablespoons honey
> ½ cup kasha
> 1 package proofable fast-rising yeast (2 teaspoons)
>   *(see yeast note, page 5)*
> ½ teaspoon sugar
> ⅛ teaspoon nutmeg
> pinch of mace
> ¼ cup warm water
> 1 egg
> 3 tablespoons oil
> ½ cup whole wheat flour
> about 1¾ cups all-purpose flour
> 1 teaspoon salt
> ½ cup raisins

1. In a small pot boil together the milk and honey. When the honey has melted pour the hot milk over the kasha in a heat-proof bowl. Cover and set aside. Sprinkle the yeast into a large mixing bowl, add the sugar, nutmeg, and mace, and

stir in the warm water. Put aside in a warm spot for about 5 minutes.

2. Add the egg and oil to the foamy yeast and beat with a wire whisk; continue whisking while adding the softened kasha. Use a wooden spoon to stir in the whole wheat flour and beat well for a full minute. Add 1 cup of the all-purpose flour and the salt and mix until the batter is well blended, then turn out onto a pastry board. Have the remaining ¾ cup of flour in a dish nearby and knead the dough for 10 minutes while adding just enough flour to make a soft, firm dough that isn't sticky. When the dough is thoroughly kneaded, lightly flour the board and throw—really throw—the dough against it fifty times.

3. Oil a mixing bowl, drop the dough into it, and flip over to grease all surfaces. Cover with a damp cloth and place in a warm spot to rise for 30 minutes.

4. Oil a loaf pan, punch down the dough, sprinkle on the raisins, and knead them in with a light hand. Gather the dough and put it into the pan. Cover and let rise again for 20 minutes.

Preheat oven to 350 degrees.

5. Bake the bread for about 30 minutes or until it sounds hollow when rapped on the bottom. Cool on a rack.

Sally Lunn

There are as many attributions for the quaint name of this sweet bread as there are research books one may consult. But almost everyone agrees that the bread is of English origin and may or may not have been sold on the streets of Bath by one Sally Lunn. There seems to be enough evidence to support the claim that the original version was a roll and not a whole bread. It is delicious eating in either form.

Makes one round 10-inch bread (1¾ pounds)

> 1 package proofable fast-rising yeast (2 teaspoons)
>   *(see yeast note, page 5)*
> ⅓ cup sugar, plus ½ teaspoon
> large pinch of nutmeg
> ¼ cup warm water
> ¾ cup milk
> ½ cup butter, cut into pieces
> 3 eggs, room temperature
> about 3½ cups all-purpose flour

1. In a large mixing bowl stir together the yeast, ½ teaspoon of sugar, and nutmeg; pour in the warm water, stir, and put aside in a warm spot for at least 5 minutes. Meanwhile, heat ½ cup of milk and the butter together until the butter melts. Pour the remaining ¼ cup cold milk and ⅓ cup sugar in a small bowl; pour in the hot buttered milk, stir, and put aside to cool.

2. Add the eggs to the foamy yeast and beat well with a wire whisk. Add 1 cup of the flour and whisk vigorously for 1 minute, then pour in the lukewarm milk. Add another 1½ cups of flour and beat hard with a wooden spoon for about 3 minutes or until a few lazy bubbles erupt when the beating is stopped. Add the remaining 1 cup of flour and beat another minute. The batter should be stiff but soft. Scrape the batter down into the bowl, cover with a towel soaked in hot water and wrung out, and put aside in a warm spot for 30 minutes.

Preheat oven to 375 degrees.

3. Thoroughly grease or oil a 10-inch gugelhupf or tube pan. Check the capacity of the pan because some are deeper than others; a 10-cup capacity is needed. Stir down the batter and scrape into the prepared mold. Tap the mold on the counter to settle the batter into all the decorative crevices. Smooth the top with a moistened spatula, cover, and put it in a warm place for 15 minutes.

4. Bake the Sally Lunn for about 35 minutes or until it is nicely puffed and well browned; it may develop a crack on top. Transfer to a rack and let cool for 10 minutes, then carefully cut around the outer edge and the center tube with a long, thin knife and reverse onto a rack to col.

Sally Lunn Rolls: Make the dough exactly the same way, but spoon into well-greased custard cups and bake for about 20 minutes. The second rise is not necessary for the rolls, which will be hot and ready to enjoy in about one hour.

Onion Rye Bread

This light rye is not overwhelmed by onion flavor, just en-
hanced by it. In fact, I discovered that if in the initial frying
the onions are cooked too long their presence all but disap-
pears. To enjoy the full flavor of this loaf, serve it warmed or
lightly toasted.

Makes one loaf (1½ pounds)

> 1 package proofable fast-rising yeast (2 teaspoons)
>   *(see yeast note, page 5)*
> 2 tablespoons sugar, plus ½ teaspoon
> large pinch of ginger
> ½ cup warm water
> 8 tablespoons butter (1 stick)
> 1 cup onions, chopped coarse
> 2 eggs
> ¼ cup dried skim milk
> 1 cup rye flour
> about 2 cups all-purpose flour
> 1 teaspoon salt

1. In a large bowl mix together the yeast, ½ teaspoon
sugar, ginger, and warm water. Stir and put aside in a warm
place. Meanwhile, melt the butter in a skillet, add the onions,
cover, and cook about 2 minutes or just until they begin to
soften; do not cook too long.

2. To the yeast bowl add 1 egg, remaining 2 tablespoons sugar, and dried milk and beat well with a wire whisk for about a minute. Add rye flour and 1½ cups all-purpose flour. Liberally flour a pastry board and knead the dough on it for 10 minutes, adding as much additional flour as necessary to make a smooth dough. Add the onions and salt and knead for 1 more minute. Oil a bowl, drop the dough into it, turn to grease all surfaces, cover with a damp cloth, and put in a warm place to rise for 30 minutes.

Preheat oven to 375 degrees.

3. Grease a loaf pan and beat the remaining egg. Punch down the dough and knead in the bowl for about 1 minute. Transfer the dough to the prepared pan, cover with a damp towel or plastic wrap, and let rise in a warm spot for 15 minutes.

4. Brush the top of the loaf with the beaten egg and bake for about 30 minutes or until it sounds hollow when rapped on the bottom. Remove to a rack to cool.

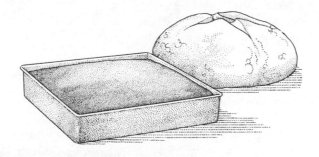

Ricotta-Herb Bread

Ricotta does not add much flavor to this tasty loaf, but it does add a sauve note. The quantity of herbs can be increased, if you wish, but do not overdo it—once baked into the bread, herbs can become overpowering.

Makes one loaf (1¾ pounds)

¼ cup milk
1 package proofable fast-rising yeast (2 teaspoons)
    (see yeast note, page 5)
¼ teaspoon sugar
pinch of ginger
2 eggs, room temperature
6 tablespoons butter, softened
1½ cups ricotta
about 3½ cups all-purpose flour
½ cup parsley
½ teaspoon dried basil
¼ teaspoon mace
2 teaspoons salt

1. Scald the milk and let cool to 115 degrees; because of the small quantity, the milk cools quickly. Put the yeast, sugar, and ginger in a large mixing bowl, add the warm milk, and stir to dissolve the yeast. Cover and put in a warm spot for 10 minutes.

2. Add the eggs and butter to the yeast sponge and whisk well to blend together. Add the ricotta and whisk again. Add 3 cups of flour and beat with a wooden spoon until the dough is smooth and slightly elastic. If the dough seems too soft, gradually add more flour until the dough has enough body but is not dry. Oil a clean bowl, gather the dough into a ball, and drop it into the bowl; turn the ball of dough over to grease all surfaces. Cover the bowl with a cloth soaked in hot water and wrung out and let rise for 30 minutes.

Preheat oven to 375 degrees.

3. While the dough is rising, oil a bread pan. Punch down the dough, add the parsley, basil, mace, and salt, and knead briefly in the bowl. Transfer the dough to the bread pan, cover, and let rise again in a warm spot for 20 minutes.

4. Bake the bread for about 50 minutes or until it sounds hollow when rapped on the bottom. Remove to a rack to cool.

Zucchini-Cheese Roll
(Food Processor)

Instead of randomly sprinkling grated zucchini and cheese over the rolled-out dough, cover half of the rectangle with each. Once rolled, the loaf has a very attractive orange and green spiral. See the note about using grated zucchini on page 64.

Makes one loaf (1½ pounds)

> about 2½ cups bread flour
> 1 teaspoon fast-rising yeast
> ½ teaspoon salt
> 1 tablespoon sugar
> pinch of ginger
> 1 cup water
> ¼ teaspoon vinegar
> 4 ounces cheddar cheese, grated
> 1 pound grated, frozen zucchini
> 1 egg, beaten

1. Follow the directions for Sandwich Bread II (Food Processor) (page 116). While the dough is rising put the frozen zucchini in a colander and run hot tap water over it until defrosted; this will take just a minute or two. A handful at a time, squeeze out all the moisture from the zucchini. Oil a loaf pan.

2. Punch down the risen dough and place it on a lightly floured work surface. Either pat with your hands or gently roll out the dough into a rectangle about 10 × 14 inches. Do not press down very hard on the dough. Brush the dough very well with the beaten egg. Sprinkle the grated cheese across half the narrower dimension of dough. On the other half, scatter the zucchini. Do not take either filling to the long edges of the dough, leave about ½ inch of clear border. Press the cheese and zucchini lightly with your hands. Sprinkle over them most of the remaining beaten egg, leaving a teaspoon or so for glazing the top.

3. Lift the narrow, cheese-covered end and tightly roll the dough. Pinch the seams closed and transfer the roll to the loaf pan, squeezing in a little to make it fit if too long. Cover with plastic wrap and put in a warm place to rise for 30 minutes.

Preheat oven to 425 degrees.

4. Just before putting the pan into the oven, brush the top with the remaining beaten egg. Bake for 10 minutes, reduce the heat to 350 degrees, and bake for about 20 minutes more. Remove the bread from the pan and rap on the bottom, if it sounds hollow, the loaf is ready. Cool on a rack.

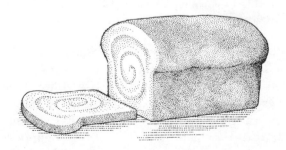

Chili-Sausage Bread

There are any number of roles that can be played by this spicy bread. It pairs beautifully with a cup of steaming coffee; makes a piquant accompaniment to cocktails; and turns a simple soup course into a hearty meal.

Makes one roll (1¼ pounds)

> ½ pound kielbasa or similar soft sausage
> ¼ to ½ cup chopped, hot green chili peppers
> 1 teaspoon proofable fast-rising yeast
> (see yeast note, page 5)
> 1 tablespoon sugar, plus ⅛ teaspoon
> pinch of ginger
> 2 tablespoons warm milk
> 4 tablespoons butter, softened
> ¼ teaspoon salt
> 2 eggs
> ¼ cup ricotta
> 1½ cups all-purpose flour

1. Remove any casing from the sausage and either shred or cut the sausage into fine pieces. Wipe a skillet with oil and place it on medium heat. Add the sausage, turn the heat to high, and fry the meat for about 2 minutes, turning it several times. (The purpose of this step is to drive out most of the fat and moisture which otherwise would exude into the dough while baking.) Place two paper towels on a dish and lift the sausage out of the skillet with a skimmer, leaving be-

hind as much liquid as possible. Cover with two more paper towels and press down on the meat; put aside. Put the chili peppers in a small strainer; the amount will depend on your taste for fire. One-quarter cup gives a mildly hot filling and half a cup is potent. Press the peppers to remove the liquid and put aside.

2. Stir the yeast, ⅛ teaspoon sugar, and ginger together in a small bowl. Pour in the milk, stir, and put aside in a warm spot. Cream the butter and 1 tablespoon sugar together in a bowl. Add the salt and 1 egg and beat until creamy. Add the ricotta and the foamy yeast and blend well into the mixture.

3. Put the flour in another bowl, make a well in the center, and pour the creamy yeast mixture into the well. With a wooden spoon, work the flour into the added ingredients beginning with the flour closest to the center, then making wider circles. Once all the flour is incorporated, beat well for 1 minute. Turn the dough onto a floured board, cover with the bowl, and let it rest for 10 minutes.

4. Roll the dough into a rectangle measuring about 18 × 10 inches. Mix the sausage and chili peppers together (you can use the same bowl used for the ricotta mixture) and spread over the dough, leaving about 1 inch clean edge all around. Starting with one narrow side, roll the dough jelly-roll fashion and transfer to a greased baking sheet, seam side down. Pinch the ends and place in a warm spot to rise for 30 minutes.

Preheat oven to 350 degrees.

5. Beat the remaining egg and brush it over the top of the roll. Bake for about 35 minutes or until the top is a deep brown or a toothpick plunged in comes out clean. Cool on a rack.

Peanut Butter Bread

It goes without saying that Peanut Butter Bread is a natural for jelly sandwiches. But because of its smooth flavor you will also find it surprisingly good for ham, cheese, or chicken sandwiches or even to enjoy straight, just for itself.

Makes one loaf (1½ pounds)

> 1 package proofable fast-rising yeast (2 teaspoons)
>   *(see yeast note, page 5)*
> ¼ cup brown sugar, packed
> ¼ cup warm water
> ¾ cup cold water
> 1 tablespoon oil
> ¼ cup peanut butter
> about 2½ cups bread flour
> 1 teaspoon salt
> ½ cup unroasted, unsalted peanuts, chopped*

1. In a small bowl mix together the yeast, half the sugar and the warm water. Put aside in a warm spot. Pour ¼ cup cold water, oil, remaining sugar, and the peanut butter into a small pot and cook over medium heat until the peanut butter melts; stir occasionally. Pour the hot liquid into a large mixing bowl and add the remaining ½ cup cold water.

2. Test the temperature of the liquid ingredients; it should not exceed 115 degrees. Scrape in the foamy yeast and 1 cup of flour and beat with a wire whisk for 1 minute. Add another

cup of flour and the salt and stir with a wooden spoon until all the ingredients are well blended. Liberally flour a pastry board and knead the dough on it for 8 to 10 minutes, adding just enough flour to make a firm, nonsticky dough that is smooth and elastic. Lightly flour the board and throw the ball of dough down hard against it fifty times. Oil a bowl, drop the dough into it, and turn it over to grease all surfaces. Cover with a towel soaked in hot water and wrung out and let rise in a warm spot for 30 minutes.

Preheat oven to 350 degrees.

3. Sprinkle the chopped nuts into the bowl, punch down the dough, and knead in the bowl for a minute. Grease a loaf pan, place the dough in it, cover, and let rise for 15 minutes.

4. Bake the bread for about 30 minutes or until it is nicely colored and a rap on the bottom sounds hollow. Remove to a rack to cool.

*Available in Oriental and health food stores.

Cottage Cheese Swirl
(Food Processor)

Even though the pale color of the cheese filling fades into the sweetened bread, the flavor snaps out at you. Only green scallion flecks hint at the creamy surprise. The rolled bread is twisted in concentric circles in a mold. The wider the mold the flatter the finished bread. My preference is for a six-inch bread which is high and handsome.

Makes one 6- to 8-inch round (1½ pounds)

BREAD:

      about 2½ cups bread flour
      1 teaspoon fast-rising yeast
      ½ teaspoon salt
      1 tablespoon sugar
      pinch of mace
      1 cup warm water
      ¼ teaspoon vinegar

FILLING:

      ½ pound small curd cottage or farmer cheese
      2 tablespoons heavy cream
      2 scallions
      ½ teaspoon ground coriander
      ¼ teaspoon nutmeg
      1 teaspoon sugar
      salt and pepper
      2 eggs, beaten

1. Prepare the dough according to the directions for Sandwich Bread II (Food Processor) (page 116), substituting mace for ginger. While the dough is rising, prepare the filling. Mash the cheese and cream together in a bowl. Trim the scallion roots and chop the entire scallions into small pieces. Add the scallions to the bowl, sprinkle in the coriander, nutmeg, sugar, salt, and pepper and stir. Reserve about 1 tablespoon of the beaten eggs for glazing the top, pour the rest into the bowl, and mix well. Grease a 6- or 8-inch round pan or soufflé dish, fit a piece of wax or parchment paper in the bottom, and grease it as well.

Preheat oven to 350 degrees.

2. Roll the dough into a rectangle about 18 × 10 inches and ¼-inch thick. Keep the wider dimension toward you. Spread the filling over the dough leaving a border about 1 inch all around. Lift the long edge nearest you and begin rolling the dough jelly-roll fashion. Press the seams and ends closed. Carefully lift the roll, which may be a bit soft, and lay it into the prepared mold beginning at the outer edge and making concentric circles toward the center. If the center is not closed, push the rings together from the outer edges until the gap is filled. Cover the mold and put it in a warm place for 15 minutes.

3. Brush the reserved egg over the surface of the swirl and bake for about 35 minutes or until it is well browned and a skewer plunged into the center of one of the rings comes out slightly moist but with no filling sticking to it. Cool the swirl in the mold for 10 minutes, turn out, and cool on a rack. It is best served warm.

Armenian Flatbread (Lavash)

There are recipes for both leavened and unleavened *lavash,* the crisp, super-thin flatbread from Armenia. Housewives there usually bake it against the walls of a clay oven; this version is not so adventurous.

Makes eight 12-inch rounds

> 1 package proofable fast-rising yeast (2 teaspoons)
>   *(see yeast note, page 5)*
> 1 tablespoon sugar
> 2 cups warm water
> about 4½ cups all-purpose flour
> 8 tablespoons butter, melted
> ½ tablespoon salt

1. In a large mixing bowl stir the yeast and sugar together and pour in the water. Stir and put aside in a warm spot for 5 minutes. Add 2 cups flour and beat vigorously with a whisk for 3 minutes. Add another 2 cups flour, the butter, and salt and beat with a wooden spoon until the batter is well blended. Gather the dough into a ball, cover the bowl with a damp cloth, and let the dough rest for 10 minutes.

2. Turn the dough onto a well-floured board and knead for 10 minutes, adding just enough flour to make a dough that is not sticky. Gather the dough into a ball and throw it against the board ten times. It should become smooth and satiny. Oil a mixing bowl, drop the dough into it, turn to

grease all surfaces, cover with a damp cloth, and put aside in a warm spot for 30 minutes or until the dough has doubled in bulk.

Preheat oven to 400 degrees.

3. Grease a sturdy baking sheet. Punch down the dough and pull apart into eight pieces. Knead one ball at a time for a few seconds, then roll out into a 12-inch circle. Often you will have fanciful shapes instead of perfect circles; all shapes are equally delicious. Transfer the thin round to the baking sheet by wrapping it onto the rolling pin and unwrapping directly onto the sheet. Bake for about 10 minutes or until the bottom is flecked with color; turn over and bake an additional minute. Remove to a rack to cool. Continue rolling and baking the rest of the balls of dough, keeping them covered with plastic wrap or a damp cloth. It is not necessary to grease the baking sheet between batches.

4. Store *lavash* in a airtight container, but if they become limp they can be recrisped in a 375-degree oven for about 3 minutes.

Rolled Orange-Raisin Bread

The look of this bread is more harmonious if white raisins are used. The soft tone blends in with the pale orange of the interior.

Makes one loaf (1½ pounds)

> 1 teaspoon proofable fast-rising yeast
>   *(see yeast note, page 5)*
> ¼ cup sugar
> pinch of allspice
> ¼ cup warm water
> ¾ cup orange juice
> 1 cup quick oatmeal
> ¼ cup dried skim milk
> Optional: ½ teaspoon orange liqueur
> 1 egg, beaten
> 2 tablespoons oil
> about 3½ cups all-purpose flour
> ¾ cup white raisins

1. Put the yeast in a small bowl with ¼ teaspoon sugar and the allspice. Add the warm water, stir, and put aside in a warm spot. Meanwhile, bring the orange juice just to the boiling point in a small pot. Have ready in a large mixing bowl the oatmeal, rest of the sugar, dried milk, and the liqueur, if desired. Stir the hot orange juice for a few seconds, then pour it over the contents in the bowl and stir well. Test the

temperature of the hot mixture; it should not be higher than 115 degrees.

2. Grease a loaf pan and put aside. Scrape the foamy yeast into the bowl containing the batter base and stir again. Add egg, oil, and 2½ cups of flour and beat vigorously with a wooden spoon until the batter pulls away from the bowl. Spread ½ cup of flour on a pastry board and knead it into the dough for 10 minutes or until the dough is smooth and elastic. Add more flour only if absolutely necessary. Let the dough rest 5 minutes while cleaning the board. Sprinkle the board lightly with flour and roll the dough into a rectangle about 16 × 10 inches. Brush the dough with warm water and sprinkle with the raisins.

3. Roll the dough tightly jelly-roll fashion, pinch the seam and the ends, and transfer to the prepared pan, seam side down. Brush with oil, cover, and let rise in a warm spot for 30 minutes.

Preheat oven to 350 degrees.

4. Bake the loaf for about 40 minutes or until nicely browned. Unmold the bread onto a rack to cool.

German Fruit Bread (Stollen)

Unlike most holiday fruit breads, this untraditional version is leavened with baking powder instead of yeast. But that does not mean it is any less authentic. A German friend brought it to these shores and still uses it every holiday season for gifts. She points out that it improves with age and can be stored, if well wrapped, up to six weeks in the refrigerator. With gifts in mind, the recipe is for two *stollen*.

Makes two *stollen* (1½ pounds each)

4½ cups all-purpose flour
1 tablespoon baking powder
½ teaspoon salt
4 tablespoons lard, cut into pieces and softened
¼ pound butter, cut into pieces and softened
1 teaspoon vanilla
⅛ teaspoon lemon extract
⅛ teaspoon almond extract
1 tablespoon rum
⅛ teaspoon ground cardamom
⅛ teaspoon nutmeg
¾ to 1 cup sugar
3 eggs
2 cups ricotta or farmer cheese
½ cup almonds, unpeeled and chopped coarse
½ cup currants
½ cup raisins
½ to 1 cup candied lemon rind, chopped

TOPPING:

1 tablespoon butter, melted
confectioners' sugar

Preheat oven to 350 degrees.

1. Sift the flour, baking powder, and salt onto a pastry board. Make a well in the center and put in it the lard, butter, vanilla, extracts, rum, cardamom, nutmeg, and sugar, the amount depending on your taste for sweetness; I prefer ¾ cup. Knead these flavorings together, then add the eggs and ricotta and knead together until the ingredients are fairly well amalgamated. Begin working in the flour, pulling a little at a time into the center. Before the dough is kneaded into a ball, add the nuts and fruits and continue kneading into a smooth dough. Alternatively, cream the lard, butter, and sugar together in a bowl; add the flavorings, eggs, and ricotta and whisk together very well. Scrape this creamed mixture into the well and little by little, work the flour into the soft ingredients.

2. Roll out half the dough into a 16 × 12-inch rectangle about 1 inch thick. The dough is now folded into thirds by lifting one of the narrow ends and folding it over two-thirds of the rectangle. Lift the remaining one-third of dough and fold it onto the package. Press lightly. Repeat with the other half of dough.

3. Place the *stollen* on a lightly greased baking sheet and bake for 1 to 1½ hours or until a skewer plunged into the center comes out dry. Transfer to a rack and brush with the melted butter and dust with confectioners' sugar. Once the fruit breads are cool, dust with confectioners' sugar again.

Nut Roll

Nut Roll is the title used here because that was always the
favorite filling around our house. My mother also used
poppy seed and apricot garnishes. This is not her traditional
recipe but a streamlined version that she graciously approves
of. Since Nut Roll is a great holiday sweet bread the recipe is
given for two loaves, one for enjoying, one for giving.

Makes two rolls (1¼ pounds each)

FILLING:

about ½ cup milk
½ pound walnuts, ground fine
5 or 6 tablespoons sugar
½ teaspoon vanilla

BREAD: have all ingredients at room temperature

¼ cup milk
1 package proofable fast-rising yeast (2 teaspoons)
    (see yeast note, page 5)
1½ tablespoons sugar
pinch of nutmeg
¼ pound butter (1 stick)
1 cup sour cream
2 eggs
3 cups all-purpose flour
½ teaspoon salt

1. Prepare the filling first. Put the milk on to boil while stirring together in a bowl the nuts, sugar to taste, and vanilla. Pour on just enough hot milk to make a paste.

2. Heat the milk until warm, about 115 degrees. Put the yeast, ½ teaspoon sugar, and the nutmeg in a small bowl. Pour the milk over the yeast, stir, and put aside in a warm place. Meanwhile, oil a baking sheet.

3. In a large mixing bowl whisk together the butter and the remaining sugar; add the sour cream and 1 egg and blend together very well with a whisk. Stir in the foamy yeast. Put the flour and salt in a sifter and gradually sift the dry ingredients into the bowl while stirring with a wooden spoon. Knead the dough in the bowl for a minute or two.

4. Break off half the dough and roll on a floured pastry board to a rectangle about 16 × 10 inches. Beat the remaining egg and brush most of it over the dough. Spread the filling over the dough without reaching to the very edges; leave about a half-inch border of dough. Lift one long edge of the rectangle and roll the dough jelly-roll fashion and place on the baking sheet, seam side down. Pinch the edges closed. Repeat with the other half of dough. Cover the two rolls with plastic wrap and put in a warm spot for 45 minutes.

Preheat oven to 350 degrees.

5. Brush the rolls with the remaining egg and bake for about 35 to 40 minutes or until well browned. Remove to a rack and cool but do not turn over and rap the bottom to test for doneness. This dough is fragile while warm. Cool before cutting.

Jam Swirl (Food Processor)

Any number of fillings can be used for this sweetened bread: nuts, poppy seed, stewed dried apricots, prune paste, or mixed chopped dried fruits. Jam is cited in the recipe because the cook who bakes on impulse can usually find some on the kitchen shelf. Here is proof positive that simple products can be used to elaborate effect.

Makes one 6- to 8-inch round bread (1½ pounds)

> about 2½ cups bread flour
> 1 teaspoon fast-rising yeast
> ½ teaspoon salt
> 2 tablespoons sugar
> pinch of ginger
> 1 cup warm water
> ¼ teaspoon vinegar
> 1 egg, beaten

FILLING:

> 1 cup jam or jelly (plum, grape, and raspberry are
>   especially good)
> 1 tablespoon fruit liqueur, preferably kirsch
> ¼ teaspoon nutmeg

1. Prepare the dough according to the directions for Sandwich Bread II (Food Processor) (page 116) using twice the amount of sugar. While the dough is rising, stir the filling in-

gredients together to soften the jam or jelly. Grease a 6- or 8-inch round pan or soufflé dish, fit a piece of wax or parchment paper in the bottom, and grease it as well.

2. Roll the dough into a rectangle about 18 × 10 inches and ¼-inch thick. Keep the wider dimension toward you. Spread the filling over the dough leaving a border of about 1 inch all around. Lift the long edge nearest you and begin rolling the dough jelly-roll fashion. Press the seams and ends closed. Carefully lift the roll, which may be a bit soft, and lay it into the prepared mold beginning at the outer edge and making concentric circles toward the center. If the center is not closed, push the rings together from the outer edges until the gap is filled. Cover the mold and put it in a warm place for 30 minutes.

Preheat oven to 350 degrees.

3. Brush the beaten egg over the surface of the swirl and bake for about 35 minutes or until it is well browned and a skewer plunged into the center of one of the rings comes out free of any dough clinging to it. Cool the swirl in the mold for 10 minutes, turn out, and cool on a rack.

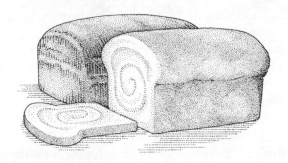

Italian Sweet Coffee Cake (Panettone)

What *pandolce* is to Genoa and *panforte* is to Siena, *panettone* is to Milan. This traditional Christmas sweet bread is one of the best-known specialties of Lombardy, and millions of packages of it are sold each December in Italy. Motta and Alemagna, the two Milanese companies that are the biggest producers of the bread, also send it around the world. The shipped product, alas, does not measure up in flavor or moisture to one bought in the shadow of Milan's great cathedral. Italian housewives who make their own *panettone* spend most of the day doing it. By considerably altering the procedure, the same delectable results can be produced in a mere two hours. Fat retards gluten from developing; for this reason the butter is added after the first rise. The time-honored way to bake *panettone* is on a buttered baking sheet with the ball of dough contained in a collar of well-buttered paper. I find a mold easier to work with.

The two different kinds of raisins, candied lemon peel, and almonds are the classic garnishes for *panettone*, but Italian housewives don't feel bound by the rules. Only one kind of raisin can be used, different nuts can be added, and other light-colored candied fruits can be substituted for the lemon. I have even used dried apricots, and my Italian friends loved it. The slightly tart flavor of the apricots and their vivid color played well against the sweetened bread. Don't use more than one cup of garnish for this amount of dough.

Makes one round loaf (2 pounds)

1 package proofable fast-rising yeast (2 teaspoons)
    (see yeast note, page 5)
¼ cup sugar, plus ½ teaspoon
large pinch of nutmeg
¼ cup warm water
½ cup milk
about 3½ cups all-purpose flour
grated rind of 1 lemon
1 teaspoon vanilla
2 eggs, room temperature, beaten
5 tablespoons butter
½ teaspoon salt
Optional: 1 teaspoon amaretto liqueur
¼ cup candied lemon peel
¼ cup dark raisins
¼ cup white raisins
¼ cup almonds, chopped

1. Mix the yeast, ½ teaspoon sugar, and nutmeg together in a small bowl, stir in the warm water, and put aside in a warm spot. Meanwhile, scald the milk and pour it into a large mixing bowl, add ¼ cup sugar and 1 cup of flour, and stir. Add the lemon rind, vanilla, and the foamy yeast and whisk all together for about 2 minutes. Add the eggs and another 2½ cups of flour and stir until all ingredients are blended. Then gently knead the dough in the bowl for about 5 minutes. This dough does not get roughed up as some others do. Scrape the dough down into the bowl with a spatula dipped in hot water, cover with a cloth soaked in hot water and wrung out, and put in a warm spot to rise for 30 minutes.

2. Meanwhile, melt 4 tablespoons of butter, cool, and add the salt and the amaretto, if desired. Chop the candied lemon peel and mix with the raisins and almonds in a small bowl. Grease a 12-cup round charlotte mold or similar pan; even a

soufflé dish will do. The shape should be round. Fit a piece of parchment paper in the bottom of the mold and grease it as well.

Preheat oven to 400 degrees.

3. Pour the melted butter over the risen dough and gently knead the dough while working the butter into it. Once the butter has been incorporated, sprinkle in the fruit and nuts and work them in. Scrape the dough into the prepared mold, cover again with a hot cloth, and put in a warm spot to rise for 20 minutes. Melt the remaining tablespoon of butter.

4. Bake the *panettone* for 10 minutes, reduce the heat to 350 degrees, and brush the top of the bread with half the melted butter. Bake another 30 to 35 minutes or until the top is well puffed, crisp, and a dark golden brown. A knife inserted into the center should come out clean. Cool in the pan on a rack for 10 minutes, turn out, and brush again with melted butter. Cool the bread on a rack. When completely cooled, cut into wedges.

Index